SAINT JOSEPH

AND THE TRIUMPH OF THE SAINTS

by
THOMAS W. PETRISKO

DEDICATION

This book is dedicated to Michael Petrisko, my uncle
"Sam." Sam was a true saint, he was simple and humble,
loving and generous. He was my best friend and
I dearly miss him.

St. Andrews Productions
6111 Steubenville Pike
McKees Rocks, PA 15136

St. Andrews Productions
Phone: (412) 787-9754
Fax: (412) 787-5204
Internet: www.saintandrew.com
Printed in the United States of America

Scriptural quotations are take from The Holy Bible —RSV:
Catholic Edition. Alternate translations from the Latin Vulgate
Bible (Douay Rheims Version —DV) are indicated when used.
Some of the Scriptural quotations from the New American
Bible: St. Joseph Edition, The New American Bible— Fireside
Family Edition 1984-1985, The Holy Bible—Douay Rheims
Edition, The New American Bible— Red Letter Edition 1986.

ACKNOWLEDGMENTS

I never planned on writing a book about St. Joseph and the saints. But beginning in the spring of 1997, I received many, many "signs" and indications that I was to write this book. I believe the Lord moved my heart because it has been prophesied for so long that St. Joseph needed to be recognized in a more prominent way before the Triumph of the Immaculate Heart would come into the world. Perhaps this book aids in that effort.

I wish to thank those most helpful to me during the writing of this book: Robert and Kim Petrisko, Dr. Frank Novasack, Fr. Richard Foley, Michael Fontecchio, Amanda DeFazio, Carole McElwain, Carol Jean Speck, Joan Smith, Jim Petrilena, Clyde Gualandri, John Haffert, Fr. Robert Herrmann, Fr. Michael O'Carroll, Joe and Sharon Ripper, Mrs. B. Laboissonniere, Sister Agnes McCormick, Mary Lou Sokol, the prayer group at the Pittsburgh Center for Peace, Fr. John O'Shea, Joe and Gerry Simboli, Jason Brunnel, and the Reverend Stanley Smolenski.

Most importantly, I thank my family for the support and sacrifice they have made for this work, my wife Emily, daughters Maria, Sarah and Natasha, and my son, Joshua. A special thank you to my mother and father, Andrew and Mary Petrisko.

ABOUT THE AUTHOR

Dr. Thomas W. Petrisko was the President of the Pittsburgh Center for Peace from 1990 to 1998 and he served as editor of the Center's five "Special Edition" newspapers. These papers, featuring the apparitions and revelations of the Virgin Mary, were published in many millions throughout the world. He is the author of *For the Soul of the Family; The Story of the Apparitions of the Virgin Mary to Estela Ruiz, The Sorrow, the Sacrifice and the Triumph; The Visions, Apparitions and Prophecies of Christina Gallagher, Call of the Ages, The Prophecy of Daniel, In God's Hand; the Miraculous Story of Little Audrey Santo, Mother of The Secret, False Prophets of Today, St Joseph and The Triumph of the Saints* and *The Last Crusade.*

Dr. Petrisko, along with his wife Emily, have three daughters, Maria, Sarah, Natasha, and a son, Joshua.

The decree of the Congregation for the Propagation of the Faith (AAS 58, 1186 - approved by Pope Paul VI on 14 October 1966) rules that the *Nihil obstat* and *Imprimatur* are no longer required for publications that deal with private revelations, apparitions, prophecies, miracles, etc., provided that nothing is said in contradiction of faith and morals.

The author hereby affirms his unconditional submission to whatever final judgment is delivered by the Church regarding the events currently under investigation in this book.

CONTENTS

FOREWORD

BY FR. RICHARD FOLEY, SJ.

St. Joseph is second only to Our Lady as the complete all-round patron in heaven. That is to say, besides being supremely holy, he is an ideal friend and advocate when we approach him in our different needs.

In the first place, St. Joseph is patron of Christ's world-wide family the Church. And this is because of his headship of the Holy Family. This further explains why he is the heavenly protector of every individual human family. Again, as the man closest to Jesus and Mary he is the model for all who strive after closer Christlikeness.

One very special need that commonly prompts young ladies to invoke St. Joseph's intercession is that he will help them find a nice husband. And, in turn, who more fittingly and effectively will assist with his prayers any young man in search of the right life-partner than "he who cherished Mary with a husband's love", as the liturgy describes him.

Another vital area over which St. Joseph is principal patron is the world of work. And with very good reason too. For it was as bread-winner for the Holy Family that he plied his trade at Nazareth. In the process he taught us to sanctify our daily labours, of whatever kind they may be.

One of the commonest and most important needs for which St. Joseph's prayers are requested is the grace of a happy death. Underlying this is the ancient tradition that he himself died at Nazareth in the presence of Jesus and Mary surely the most privileged ever situation for anybody leaving this world. Hence the unique value of St. Joseph's patronage in our last moments.

Enjoying as he does such an extra-special status, and playing such a many-sided role in salvation history, St. Joseph has been adopted as their special patron by many a future saint. For they understood better than most how intimately he was locked into the life and lifework of the Redeemer and His Mother. Indeed, St. Teresa of Avila even suggested that none of us can afford the luxury of not having a devotion to Mary's spouse and foster-father of the Word made Flesh.

Dr. Petrisko's excellent work will certainly help readers to understand St. Joseph better and to approach him with the deepest confidence.

INTRODUCTION

ST. JOSEPH AND THE COMING TRIUMPH OF THE SAINTS

The diminutive, frail nun who was born in Europe but who became an Indian citizen during her six decades on the subcontinent carried claim to the title like no one else alive. For decades, even the secular media unhesitatingly declared it—Mother Teresa, the founder of the Missionaries of Charity in Calcutta, India, who ministered to the sick, the poor, and the dying, was a "living saint."

Bowed by age and declining health, her wrinkled face came to be unmistakenly recognized as a symbol of faith, hope, and kindness in a world where few would dare to make such a claim. She was everyone's hero in our materialistic, violence-marred age—an age that desperately needed her presence. And with her death, the world mourned loud and strong. Pope John Paul II succinctly capsulized Mother Teresa's life when he celebrated Holy Mass for her intention on September 6, 1997:

> In the face of those in misery she recognized
> Jesus' face, imploring from the cross 'I AM
> THIRSTY.' And with generous surrender of
> the self, she listened to the cry from the lips
> and hearts of the dying, of abandoned little
> ones, of men and women crushed by the
> weight of suffering and loneliness.

1

> Tirelessly traveling the paths of the entire world, Mother Teresa has marked the history of our century: she defended life bravely, she served all human beings, always promoting their dignity and respect; she made 'the losers of life' feel the tenderness of God, the loving Father of all His creatures. She bore witness to the Gospel of charity, which is nourished by the free giving of the self until death. This is how we remember her, invoking for her the prize that awaits all the faithful servants of the Kingdom of God.
>
> May her shining example of charity serve as a consolation and a catalyst for her spiritual family, for the Church, and for all humanity.

While the Holy Father does not intend to rush Mother Teresa's canonization, the irony that so many eagerly sought to grant the Nobel Prize-winning nun her halo is unmistakable.

"SAINTHOOD NOW?" read the cover of *Newsweek* magazine a week after Mother Teresa's death. Inside the magazine, the accompanying article was titled "Requiem for a Saint," with religious editor Kenneth L. Woodward painstakingly bemoaning the lengthy process the Church must undertake to declare those worthy of sainthood: "In most cases the road to canonization is long—50 years is average, though many take a century or more—and complicated. As Pope, John Paul II has the power to waive the process and proclaim Mother Teresa a Saint. Will he?" Likewise, *Newsweek's* Andrew Greely offered that, from personal experience, he could vouch that Mother Teresa was truly a living saint:

Saints, Real Saints, are magical. They are luminous transparent, irresistible. They enchant us, enthrall us, captivate us. They seem to be qualitatively different from the rest of humankind. They attract us not by preaching, much less by screeching, but by radiant goodness, irrepressible cheerfulness and devastating love. We are compelled to follow them, not because of what they say but because of who they are. Our aim is not necessarily to do what they do but, rather, to try to be what they are. So I discovered one, hot June afternoon during the late 1960s as I rode in a southern Ohio cab for an hour with Mother Teresa.

Such attention by the secular press with heavenly concerns flowed in the early weeks of September 1997. For just one week before Mother Teresa's death, the world experienced the tragic and untimely loss of Britain's Princess Diana.

The former Diana Spencer, who married and divorced Prince Charles, was killed in a car accident in Paris on August 31, 1997. Her death, even more than Mother Teresa's, caused millions worldwide to watch television, as the meaning of her life was rehashed over and over. Like Mother Teresa, Diana was loved by millions. Her death and funeral generated an electronically stimulated hysteria that enraptured people for more than a week.But only two hours after Princess Diana's death, *CNN*, the worlds largest television news network, began interviewing individuals who, in their genuine desire to translate Diana's life and death into something more meaningful, were calling the Princess a saint. During the following days, such speculations continued, for Diana's vast and unselfish humanitarian efforts deserved a fitting tribute.

And those struggling to define it all for the masses kept repeating the "S" word. In fact, even before Diana was buried, poorly printed T-shirts hit the streets for $8 each. They featured Diana's picture and the slogan, "Born a Princess, Died a Saint."

Then Mother Teresa, the living *"Saint of the Gutters,"* died. And suddenly, even the secular press felt in true conscience that it would be unfair to compare the lives of the two with the same moniker.

While strong opinions surfaced on which of the two women deserved to be designated a saint, it wasn't long before it became apparent that such talk didn't do justice to either of them. In life, the Princess of Wales and the octogenarian nun, simply known as "Mother," actually became great friends and mutual admirers. They truly respected and loved each other, and only weeks before, they had met again in New York City. Now, in death, both deserved fair tribute. But, certainly, Diana had never tried to appeal for acceptance into such a lofty club as heaven's holy elite. And Mother Teresa consistently rejected talk of her sainthood and had pleaded that it be put to rest once and for all.

But though it is safe to say that all comparisons between the two should be dismissed, talk of what makes a saint, and perhaps what doesn't, should not. Indeed, such talk is actually long overdue.

In a century that certainly holds claim to a legion of unholy villains, despots, and dictators, talk of true saints has been rare. Succumbing to the influence of global journalism and entertainment—which panders to and promotes secular heroes primarily from the glittery worlds of cinema, sports, fashion, business, and politics—the world has lost touch with what real heroic lives of virtue and faith are all about.

Encounters in Scripture with the lives of SS. Peter and Paul and the Apostles prevent most Christians from becoming completely detached from the concept of sainthood. And certainly, even non-Christians have crossed paths with the lives of such recognized Catholic immortals as St. Patrick, St. Francis, St. Joan of Arc, and St. Thérèsa of Liseaux. But for the most part, where have all the saints gone?

They've disappeared, thanks to today's mass communication network, which seeks to illuminate heroes of accomplishment, beauty, and intelligence, while disdaining, ridiculing, and denying that lives dedicated to upholding and defending the Gospel of Jesus Christ have any significant merit.

Indeed, the irony of it all is astounding, for what has more value, relevance, and importance than being recognized through one's life and work as a true friend of God and a true friend of man. Even the Hindus, who worship a variety of gods and goddesses, couldn't help but associate Mother Teresa's life with God.

Non-Christians throughout India and the world saw in Mother Teresa someone whose life inspired contemplation of a higher order. In her own words, Mother Teresa saw Jesus Christ in everyone, and thus her love for her Savior caused her to reach out to all, especially the poor.

Christ made it clear. Those who fed, clothed, and welcomed the least, the downtrodden, and the imprisoned were in reality, comforting Him. But along with such great and noble efforts, the Lord also said there was more merit in turning the other cheek than in striking back. That it is more important to love God than to love one's self. And that to forgive and forget paves the way for God to do the same for us on

Judgment Day.

In these time-proven truths and the faith that Jesus Christ is truly the Son of God—the Redeemer of fallen mankind—we discover what constitutes a saint. For if through prayer and discipline we can master such a life, then we will have stored in heaven a fortune that, the Lord assures us, will not be susceptible to moths, thieves and decay.

While for the last two decades the name of Calcutta's Mother Teresa has evoked the idea of sainthood, we must strain to conjure up additional names which have such exalted status. Honorable, loving, and good intentioned sorts, such as Princess Diana, emerge here and there. Their eulogies seek to gratify and honor their efforts and name. But rare in today's world, except in regards to Pope John Paul II, is there talk of those destined to be saints.

The darkness of our times is clearly seen in this glaring shortage of legitimate candidates for heaven's highest honors. We live in a world where evil has so contaminated the entire planet that our heroes are literally anti-heroes. Today's role models are individuals who personify the world's values and pleasures. They are men and women who madly quest for materialism, pleasure, and power. Indeed, it's as if we honor those today whose personal lifestyles reflect or contribute to a culture without God—those who exhibit unbridled egoism and who publicly flaunt their hunger for adulation, their disregard for purity, and their defiance of all existing moral order.

Most tragically, today's heroes of sin and vice are not only highly visible, but they are thriving and growing. For the media exploits their lifestyles to such a degree that endless admirers are emerging in imitation. Because of television, young and old alike are now fed a steady diet of anti-heroes,

little anti-christs who are collectively destroying mankind—
the mankind created in the image of God.

And so, the question arises—where is God in all of this?
Why doesn't He do something? And where are all His saints,
those that the Church proclaims God "lifts up" with each
generation?

With evil now institutionalized worldwide, the cry of the
innocent and the prayers of the faithful both plead with God
for justice. Like the days when Christ Himself walked the
earth, God-fearing people everywhere have come to believe
that perhaps our world can only be saved through divine
intervention. Indeed, like the Jews who hoped Christ would
prove to be a conquering, liberating messiah, many of today's
most faithful seem to be looking and almost hoping for one
quick strike from heaven to end the demonic strangle-hold on
the human race. Realizing that a great chastisement has been
prophesied for quite some time, this thinking embraces a
quick-fix solution to end the snowballing madness that now
covers the planet.

But in Christian history, has this ever been the path that God
has chosen to bring back His people? From the horrors of
Rome to the great dangers the Moslem invasions posed to
Christian Europe over the centuries, from the darkest, most
hopeless nights of WWII, to the world-ending potential of the
dangers of the "Cold War," has there ever come an
extraordinary, totally divine intervention to save the good and
just from the cohorts of hell?

The answer is no, for this is not God's way. God *is* going to
act in a very powerful, unparalled way in our times, but His
intervention will not deny His people the opportunity to bring
Him glory in the most glorious of ways. Indeed, it seems
undeniable that God permits events to appear all but hopeless

before He decides to act. Against great odds, surrounded in dense darkness, the history of the Church, and the entire history of good vs. evil, is one of eternal vigilance, perseverance, and patience. It is one of unceasing faith and hope in He who is the King of Kings, the Lord of Lords. It is one of confident assurance that the Good Shepherd will never abandon his sheep, yet alone permit the gates of hell to prevail. And in His time, all will be made right and just.

The Father, the Son, and Holy Spirit guide history down a certain path to the final victory. And it is this promise, destined to be fulfilled through the will and grace of God, that becomes alive and visible in His chosen souls at the chosen time.

In our world, that time is now! As with previous junctures in history, all hope seems to be gone. But God will now, through a legion of saints that He has placed on earth, both visible and hidden, bring down the evil that is swallowing the planet. Once again, as in the past, when the fate of the Christian world seems to teeter on the edge of oblivion, a great triumph will come.

A voice of confidence in this hope comes today from a soul certainly marked for sainthood. Over and over, like St. John the Baptist's cry heralding the coming of the Messiah, Pope John Paul II proclaims the dawn of a new springtime for the world and the Church.

As he staggers under the weight of his own cross, reassuring the world that our culture of death will give way to a culture of life, Pope John Paul II has repeatedly foretold the coming victory of God. Victory is certain, he proclaims, and with it will come peace, true peace for a world that hungers for such a gift.

Around the world, God's chosen ones, his intimate vessels of love that hear and relay his words and the words of the Blessed Virgin Mary, proclaim that a "Second Pentecost" is imminent. The Holy Spirit is about to descend and purify the Church and the world, the visionaries say, and all mankind must be prepared. Through an extraordinary gift of grace, today's prophets foretell that the Spirit of God, in a sweeping and powerful action, will open minds and hearts to the light of truth. And with the truth, the world will experience the greatest miracle of Divine Mercy.

However, the work at hand is just beginning. It will not be a divine strike of vengeance that crushes human will and erases evil in the blink of an eye. We must remember the First Pentecost, when the Apostles and disciples were filled with the Holy Spirit. God did not reveal His power within them until they had emerged from the Upper Room and went out among the people to do His work. Indeed, we know they changed the face of the earth forever. And so it will be again.

Soon, a great grace will be given to mankind. The Holy Spirit is about to give the world His full and perfect witness to Jesus Christ. We must recall the words of the prophet Joel, which St. Peter shared with Apostles:

> It shall come to pass in the last days, says God, that I will pour out a portion of my spirit on all mankind:
> Your sons and daughters shall prophesy, your young men shall see visions and your old men shall dream dreams.
> Yes, even on my servants and handmaids I will pour out a portion of my spirit in those days, and they shall prophesy.
> I will work wonders in the heavens above and signs on the earth below:

> blood, fire, and a cloud of smoke.
> The sun shall be turned to darkness and the
> moon to blood before the coming of that great
> and glorious day of the Lord. Then shall
> everyone be saved who calls on the name of
> the Lord (Joel 3:1-4, Acts 2:17-21).

From the words of the Prophet Joel, we understand that heaven and earth will unite in an extraordinary way—a way that will complete and fulfill mankind's salvation history. And God, through the Mystical Body of Jesus Christ, His Church, will unleash torrents of grace to produce such holiness in souls that, as it is foretold, some of the greatest saints in history will only now come forth to earn their crowns.

They will be great because God is great. And it is God who will lead them in their extraordinary efforts which, in the end, will produce the collapse and defeat of evil. From one end of the world to the other, evil is going to be brought down. Not just some evil, but according to God's holy voices, all evil! Thus, from Communism to Masonry, from organized crime to the demonic forces of contraception and abortion, the world is to be reclaimed for God. And by the strength, courage, and even the blood of Christ's soldiers, a new humanity will emerge.

While our imaginations soar in attempting to understand how this will be, we need only to look at Bernini's Colonnade, the Facade of St. Peter's Basilica in Rome, to find the answer. The two colonnades, named after the great Baroque architect, Gian Lorenzo Bernini, are made up of 140 columns which line the borders of St. Peter's Square. Impressive as the towering columns are, it is the dramatic double procession of saints that sit atop the Colonnade which inspires such indescribable awe. The 140 saints, each sculptured over three meters tall, lead to the statues of the Redeemer and the Apostles, which are positioned at the top of St. Peter's facade.

The sight of so many of the Church's luminous stalwarts aligned together and towering overhead from the Colonnade is like a visible manifesto of the Church's response to Christ's words, "Go, therefore, and make disciples of all nations" (Mt 28:19). Indeed, it took the heroic action of an untold number of saints to spread the Church to the four corners of the world—and it was not only those who adorn the Colonnade. Now in our crucial times, there can be no doubt that while God will provide the grace and the direction, and even many miraculous acts, He is also waiting for those who have heard His call to take their place among the Church's immortal heroes.

To accompany heaven's call to glory, the Church and Our Lady have not hesitated to point to the saints of the past and their heroic struggles. In her apparitions, the Blessed Virgin Mary has often been accompanied by or has spoken of the great saints. Indeed, Pope John Paul II has beatified and canonized more saints than any Pope in history. It is also not surprising that many of the great mystics and visionaries of the last two hundred years have also reported visitations from the saints.

Today, one great saint has surfaced above all others as the ultimate model for service of God. And that saint is St. Joseph, Christ's earthly father and the spouse of the Blessed Virgin Mary.

From the beginning, the Church encouraged devotion to its founding fathers, SS. Peter and Paul, and many of the other privileged souls in Scripture who were believed to be among the Blessed. This included souls such as St. John the Baptist, St. Stephen, and St. Luke. But it wasn't until the 14th century that reasons for honoring St. Joseph were explored in scholarly treatises. Later, St. Teresa of Avila extolled St. Joseph's many merits in a special way. From then on, popular devotion to St. Joseph progressed steadily, with many of the great pontiffs offering honorable tribute.

The role of St. Joseph, who is identified in the Gospels as a quiet, obedient instrument of God's divine plan, has been ever expanding. While the Church recognizes a litany of tasks that he, by merit of his own role, is worthy to be called upon for intercession, the mystics of the last five centuries have given us even more profound insight into who this extraordinary man truly was. For St. Joseph is revealed by them as being a soul that exhibited and practiced Christian virtues and behavior long before Christ Himself was born. Although Jewish scripture never taught of Christ's law of love and forgiveness, St. Joseph's life is said to have been a model for living according to Christ's teachings in Scripture.

The Venerable Mary of Agreda and other mystics say that, truly, St. Joseph was prepared by God through special graces to be the earthly father of Jesus Christ. And because of his resolute will and faith, he is today perhaps the perfect model of a father and a saint—a model the world now needs desperately.

Likewise, there are also the extraordinary prophecies that surround St. Joseph and God's coming victory. For it is said that the world must come to know and understand just who St. Joseph was and is before the Triumph will occur. Indeed, Joseph's presence at two of the Church's approved apparitions, Knock and Fatima, clearly indicates God's desire for today's Christian world to acknowledge St. Joseph.

In such tumultuous times, we must now, more than ever, respond in imitation of St. Joseph and all the saints. We must go forward like St. Joan of Arc, and with confidence, claim God's victory. And like this Patron Saint of France, with this victory in hand we will proceed to crown Our Mother and our Lord, so that their Two Hearts can reign forever until the end of time.

CHAPTER ONE

COME THE SAINTS

The darkness of our times certainly serves as inspirational fuel for innumerable essays on why today's world has no peer in moral degeneracy. "We are at rock bottom," the commentaries declare. "We are at the lowest point permitted by God without having to experience His wrath," religious leaders roar. Many say that not even in the days of Noah did the world figure out how to commit so much sin. Perhaps even Babylon would blush.

But like previous generations known for shameful levels of moral decay, the irony of the richness of life during our times is unmistakable. Like ancient Rome, 12th century China, and the Aztec culture of the little Middle Ages, our culture is at a pinnacle in technology, health care, and overall standard of living. Especially in the West, true deplorable poverty has almost disappeared. For the most part, the poor in the West possess many nonessentials, such as telephones, televisions, refrigerators, automobiles, etc. They are also able to receive health care and to be governmentally assisted in their basic needs, whether it be food or occupational training.

All of this brings us to the immortal words of Charles Dickens, for our late 20th century may be the ideal reflection of his classic prose, "it was the best of times, it was the worst of times." The world of Charles Dickens obviously possessed the same paradoxical qualities, although it could probably be said that if the renowned British author could see our world today, he would hastily retract his words in order to reissue them now with greater confidence in their intended meaning.

Indeed, the world's accelerated downward slide from the 19th Century of Charles Dickens to today is undeniable. But it is no mystery. Mankind has driven the cart down the road of total demise, becoming saturated with secularism and moral disorder—and embracing the attack on life itself. It is, as Pope John Paul II noted in *Evangelium Vitae*, an attack on God Himself.

But though Dickens probably would not have imagined that it could get much worse, it somehow has. The most mysterious variable in all of this is time. For time keeps marching forward, recording each generation's escalating sorrows and glories with no end in sight.

Scholars say that most of today's problems took root more than four hundred years ago during the Renaissance and the Age of Enlightenment. This period saw the philosophical beginnings of secularism take hold. Secularism is the belief that reality should be determined without reference to religious systems. At the intellectual level, it becomes rationalism, and at the level of life, it becomes humanism.

In essence, humanists want the world to believe that life is a mystery, a never ending puzzle that has no absolute solution or truth. They use the knowledge explosion of the last two centuries as evidence to support their position. Humanists hopefully believe that if people accept the premise that there is no absolute truth, then there can be no absolute moral laws. Everything becomes relative. According to rationalists, this then makes individual freedom the highest priority. Doing our own thing becomes more important than doing the right thing, because, in essence, there is no right thing. Pope John Paul II even warned a Jesuit audience about how relativism "leads to an unfounded primacy of freedom over truth."

Ironically, as God would have it, we actually become more

and more free as we obey the truth. This is, as John Paul II said, "The splendor of truth." At the same time, Fr. George Rutler says, we also realize "that relativism is the attempt to realize unreality," or non-truth. It especially sets aside, says Fr. Rutler, the incarnation of Christ—this "is not thinking at all, it is feeling without thinking."

And this is where the world is today. It is being lead in almost every area by those who incorporate feeling without thinking. It is a world that over-values sentiment and leads men to pursue the false virtue of pleasure.

Almost all decadent cultures of the past have self-destructed in this way. For such action creates an identity crisis. People in their pursuit of self-comfort and self-indulgences, in their pursuit of luxuries and abuses of the flesh, begin to sanctify abuse and death for the sake of compromise. Most of all, this leads people to question the existence of the true God, especially in their rush to create false gods with false laws that pander to their decadence.

Over time, history shows that this leads to horrible crimes against humanity. Dissidents become philosophically unacceptable and places like Auschwitz are not too far off the horizon.

However, all is not lost.

Philosophers today say that it appears our age is seeing the peak of moral relativism. They say the move away from truth has now gone so far that it is creating a clear "unreality." Likewise, while the daunting amount of information at our disposal today seems to be just one more instrument in the hands of the humanists to help them shape an atheistic world, it is actually this phase which will now do the opposite. With information, comes truth, and truth can't but help point to

God, His laws, and eventually His love.

Leaving the world of the mind and senses to understand this, Scripture has long foretold how the course of time would see mankind slowly come to a date with destiny. That at some point, when secular humanism and paganism appeared to reign supreme, it would then be destroyed once and for all by the One who has been given full authority in heaven and on earth.

Thus, if the great thinkers of our times see the end coming for secularism, and if at the same time God's Spirit appears to be announcing the dawn of a new age, we need only to realize that great times are at our doorstep. Indeed, we are truly crossing the "threshold of hope," as Pope John Paul II proclaims. All we need now is to wait for the blessed individuals who are destined to collide with the events of our time. For history is about to reveal today's saints before our very eyes. Yes, the saints are about to come marching in.

And these individuals promise to be special. For all authentic renewal is of the saints. Indeed, these will be the men and women who God has deemed to bring down the evil of our day. They will be uncompromising and of decidedly different character. They will need no prodding to get done what needs to be done. They will be prayerful and of singular resolve. Their mission will be to serve God, and disobedience, bad news, and negativity will not dissuade them.

Most of all, they will recognize that the world is suffering from a spiritual crisis. And they will respond to this crisis in a Christ-like manner—they will see what has to be done and they will do it. They will be fearless, for they know they march in with all the heroes of the Bible. Indeed, they will be a new light in the world, the light of a new dawn. Through the grace of God, they will be exactly what the world has been waiting for to bring about its liberation.

St. Peter

CHAPTER TWO

THE MAKING OF SAINTS

The death of Mother Teresa of Calcutta brought into focus the desperate need for saints in these times. Her life, her work, her testimony to Jesus Christ as the driving force behind both, illustrate and underscore this need. The world of the late 20th century needs its saints to shine forth. It urgently needs men and women of the Church, already chosen by God before all time, to heroically seize the moment and their destiny.

Are they here? Are they at work? Or is there a crisis of saints in our age?

Of course there is a crisis of saints! But God will not permit this to continue. For as so many brave men and women emerged during critical moments in the past, so it will be again. Throughout history, especially during the great crises that have threatened the Church and the world, God has always provided.

But before we look closer at the needs of our times, it is important to understand just what constitutes a saint and how the Church came to recognize the Causes of Saints.

There will always be heroic, recognizable figures who are chosen by God to earn their crown in the spotlight of the world. But it is the little ones, the "anawim" or "little nobodies," referred to in Scripture, who are also called to participate in God's plan for the salvation of the world. These are hidden, insignificant, humble little saints that are forever crushed by the powers of the world. United with Christ, they are really His chosen ones. Over the centuries, they have constituted a great army dedicated to prayer and suffering and are, the Virgin Mary reveals, the cornerstone of God's coming triumph in the world. This should not be surprising, for this is how the Causes of the Saints all began hundreds of years ago.

Today, the Church proclaims that the opportunity for sainthood is available to all, regardless of a person's place in life. But for every Joan of Arc, there have been perhaps thousands of saints who will never be known. This fact is especially noted in the earliest history of the Church, where we discover that the very criteria for what constitutes a saint was established through the recognition of the many heroic, invisible, and uncelebrated heroes of the early Church.

The Church couldn't help but realize that God was working in these souls. And that brings us to an interesting point—the Church doesn't make saints, God does. Scripture tells us that "this is God's will, our sanctification" (Thes 4:3). Indeed, all holy attributes and heroic virtues come from the grace of Jesus Christ. This is an unconditional reality for the saints.

Likewise, Scripture makes it clear: "You did not choose me, but I chose you." (Jn 15:16). With this truth, the Congregation for the Causes of the Saints acknowledges that while a servant of God's reputation may be based on martyrdom or heroic virtue, it is the Holy Spirit who alone raises up models of true sanctity among the faithful.

For the most part, the concept of sainthood began with the "Cult of the Martyrs and Confessors" in the early Church. By the 4th century, martyrdom became recognized as a sign of heroic virtue and sanctity among the faithful. These were the brave men and women who died in defense of the Faith. These were men and women recognized as having so totally submitted to the will of God in their lives, that they were willing to die for Him. Often, suffering and persecution accompanied their choice.

While there are various technicalities that specifically define the act of martyrdom for the faith, the earliest martyrs were primarily those who shed their blood in defense of their belief in Jesus Christ. This sacrificial act was then understood to be in union with Christ's sacrifice on the Cross. Thus, the choice of martyrdom is an act of obedience to the Lord and recalls His words: "Whoever would save his life will lose it, and whoever loses his life for my sake, he will save it" (Lk 9:24), and "Greater love has no man than this, that a man lay down his life for his friends" (Jn 15:13).

Because of the many persecutions under a string of Roman emperors, the cult of the martyrs grew and stretched out over the centuries in the early Church. Throughout the Roman empire, thousands of early Christians made the supreme sacrifice by sword, starvation, inhuman tortures, and Roman "sport."

After the Council of Nicea in 325, martyrdom at the hands of the Romans began to diminish. At that time, the early Church conducted no formal investigations of these events and individuals. But local communities of Christians began to elevate their fallen brethren in spontaneous acts of respect and honor, causing the local church to often permit veneration of a particular martyr of the faithful. Certain traditions also developed, such as the veneration and preservation of a martyr's relics and special burials under or above a church altar. Anniversary Masses also came to be celebrated, as the rise of feast days was now beginning to take hold in the Church. According to Michael Freze, S.F.O., in his book, *The Making of Saints* (Our Sunday Visitor Publishing Division, 1991), one of the first saints to be remembered through a commemorative feast day was St. Polycarp:

> One of the earliest examples of the faithful's celebrating a martyr's feast day is the case of St. Polycarp (69-155). After his death, a cult developed around him at Smyrna. Although fear of exaggerated devotion influenced the magistrate to avoid this possibility by burning his body, nevertheless Smyrneans gathered his bones, venerated them, and vowed to celebrate his annual feast day thereafter. (*Martyrium Polycarpi.* trans. J.B. Lightfoot. Chpt. 18)

> This is one of the first known annual commemorations in the Western Church of any saint, martyr or not. It is also one of the first cases when a day of martyrdom—the feast day or heavenly birthday of a saint—was recognized. Eventually, this annual commemoration would occur during the celebration of the Eucharist at the site of the Martyr's grave, which often served as an altar for the celebration. In time, the altars of the churches and basilicas took the place of the grave site as the resting place of the venerated saints.

By the middle of the 3rd century, Church authorities were beginning to authorize clergy to keep documentaries of the martyrs and of their time of death. This then led to local calendar's that commemorated the local martyrology each year.

As the Church grew, each region began to have its own martyrology, with some names crossing over to several regions. By the 6th century, a collection of liturgical readings in memory of the martyrs was begun by Dionysius Exiguus. While only read privately at first, by the 8th century, Pope Adrian I authorized what was known as the reading of the *Passion of the Martyrs* in the entire universal Church.

All of this was not without opposition. Because respect was being paid to the dead through such activities of the faithful, critics denounced everything from the manner in which relics were obtained (first class relics are composed of the saint's bones or hair) to the unworthiness of certain candidates. Gradually, proof of miraculous intercessions was also required along with martyrdom in order to grant ecclesiastical cult to the servant of God.

While the early martyrs are recognized as the initial impetus for the beginning of the Causes of the Saints, a second class of saints known as the "confessors" also existed. These were the faithful that lead holy pious lives of devotion. They imitated Christ without dying, and were seen as great role models for Church members.

Beginning in the 4th century, "confessors" became the focus of the faithful as martyrdom was slowly coming to end. Thus, the Church, according to Michael Freze, recognized that another form of sanctity was in its midst and needed to be nurtured and developed:

> The faithful soon focused upon those holy souls in their midst who no longer died for their faith; they began to observe how these pious souls actually lived their faith lives on a day-to-day basis. Martyrdom now was looked upon as a lifetime of patient, heroic suffering in the midst of uncertainty, turmoil, and fear. Even in the mundane, everyday

circumstances of life, did the faithful Christians follow the teachings of the Gospel? Did he or she strive to imitate the life of Christ, even before His Passion and death on a cross? How did they treat their neighbor and their enemy? These and many similar questions led the Church to look upon a different type of sanctity in their midst: that of the early Confessors, who 'confessed' God to the people in a heroic way. These heroic figures gave witness to Christ and His teachings by imitating His earthy life in an exemplary fashion. Many confessors became great preachers and evangelists. Some became apologists, that group of preachers and writers who defended the teachings of the faith against the heresies that flourished in those first few centuries. Arianism, Montanism, Pelagiansm, Valentinianism, Gnosticism, etc. Their goal was to defend the orthodox teachings of the Church and to uphold her sacred traditions.

It was up to the local bishop again to survey and assess the cult of the "confessor." And as with the martyrs, miracles before or after a candidate's death were considered as divine confirmation.

But it was not until the 7th century that documents supported the Church's use of the term "confessor." In these records, confessors were said to be "bold", "fearless," "enduring," and "imitations of Christ."

Because of abuses such as contrived martyrdom or questionable "confessors," the Church over time had to adopt a document process that meticulously examined a candidate's life. This took into account all of the person's virtues, deeds, motivations, acquaintances, etc. In addition, the path to approved sainthood required developmental stages that ushered a candidate's cause along a path which lead from beatification to canonization.

In these steps, the life of a candidate became scrupulously examined. It also became generally recognized that one had to be humble, pious, and virtuous. And often, if there were writings, these were also closely examined.

Today, to raise individuals to the altars of the Church, two different kinds of evidence are considered and two in-depth, complicated investigations are carried out, usually for a period of many years.

All of this can only begin after the person considered has been dead for five years. The Ordinary Process is then initiated by the local bishop. Upon being approached by individuals or a group concerning such a person, the bishop appoints a tribunal and it begins collecting evidence. He also takes testimony, favorable and unfavorable, from those who knew the candidate. If after reviewing all this evidence the Bishop is convinced of the candidate's holiness, he then forwards it all to Rome with his endorsement.

The Congregation for the Causes of Saints then begins its own review. It gathers further evidence and, if necessary, examines the person's writings. When the congregation receives a "cause," a Postulator and a Relator are appointed. The Postulator guides the case to its completion and accentuates the individual in a positive light. When he is done, the Relator sends it to other experts if needed.

Finally, the cause is delivered to a panel of nine theologians who weigh the case and then vote. If six are in affirmation, the cause goes to a larger assembly of cardinals and bishops. If by a two-thirds margin they are in approval, the cause is then presented to the Pope. However, one miracle is needed for beatification and one miracle is also need for canonization. Usually these are "medical miracles." But the Pope may waive the miracle in the case of a martyr.

CHAPTER THREE

THE SCIENCE OF THE SAINTS

What the Church deems necessary for sainthood is clearly defined. While the process evolved and matured over the centuries, the objective remained the same. Did the candidate's life produce—according to Church doctrine, traditions and practices—the necessary evidence to earn for the candidate an authentic reputation for sanctity? And if so, was it to the degree that the candidate's life deserved to be a true model for the faithful to imitate?

As the Church today clearly understands what is necessary to determine sainthood, we can refer to this process as the "science of the saints." In focusing on this objective process, however, we may fail to emphasize one of the greatest sources of defining what it means to be a saint—the thoughts and words of the saints themselves on the subject of sainthood.

Indeed, the thoughts and words of the saints provide us with a reservoir of wisdom that is unmatched in its sincerity and perspective. This is because many of the great saints truly desired to be "great saints." This desire was not prideful, for their desire to rise above the world in perfection and love of God reflected no sinful ambition but rather Christ's call to be "perfect as your Father in heaven is perfect"(Mat 5:48).

Undoubtedly, this is wisdom not pride. Wisdom is the great gift of the Holy Spirit and is responsible for the unusual awareness that saints have for their mission in life. Likewise, the saints almost always bathe in the gift of understanding. Together with wisdom, these charisms permit the profound truths of God to permeate their intellect and will, which then flow easily into their actions.

Humility, purity, and simplicity of heart together permit the saints to "see as God sees." And with this knowledge the saints then become extremely aware of their own sins and the sins of the world. Together, all of the gifts of the Holy Spirit permit the saints to act with determination and conviction. And regardless of how much the world may come to despise, marginalize, ridicule or ignore their efforts, they maintain that their work is not of themselves, but of God. Indeed, they trust in Divine Providence, which leads them through the valleys to the mountaintops in pursuit of justice. Thus, their own words, which reflect their deep understanding of who they are and why they do what they do, reveal to us in an special way what makes a saint.

St. Thérèse of Lisieux (1873-97) tells us that "you cannot be half a saint—you must be a whole saint or no saint at all." This, then, is not a part-time job. It's all or nothing, for as St. Louis de Montfort writes, "God alone in every cell of me, God alone for all eternity."

Yes, one must hunger with their entire being to be a saint. This means the body, the mind, the emotion, and the soul are fused in a harmony that explodes in optimum performance each day for the cause of God. St. Francis de Sales (1567-1622) suggests that we "look at the examples given by the saints in every walk of life. There is nothing that they have not done in order to love God and to be His devoted followers."

But the saints clearly point out that this singular purpose in their life actually comes from God, not from themselves. St. Thérèse of Lisieux explains this critical concept: "I always feel the bold confidence of becoming a great saint because I don't count on my merits, since I have none, but I trust in Him who is Virtue and Holiness. God alone, content with my weak efforts, will raise me to Himself and make me a Saint, clothing me in His infinite merits."

Similarly, St. Isidore of Seville (560-656), says that "the whole science of saints consists in knowing and following the Will of God." And, likewise, St. Alphonsus Liguori (1696-1787) proposes that "the science of the Saints is to know the love of God."

Indeed, to understand the will and love of God is essential for sainthood. But how does one grow in this grace when it is granted by God? The saints say the process along this road has to be aided and strengthened by prayer, deep prayer from the heart.

"Was it not in prayer," writes St. Thérèsè, "that St. Paul, St. Augustine, St. John of the Cross, St. Thomas Aquinas, St. Francis, St. Dominic, and so many other famous friends of God have drawn out the divine science which delights the greatest geniuses? What Archimedes was not able to obtain, for his request was not desired by God and was only made from a material viewpoint, the saints have obtained in all its fullness."

Likewise, St. Alphonsus Liguori could not emphasize enough the essential need for prayer: "The whole lives of the saints have been one of meditation and prayer. All the graces by means of which they have become Saints were received by them in answer to their prayers." This great doctor of the Church specifically outlines an approach to saintly life:

31

If we truly desire to become Saints, let us resolve: 1) to avoid every venial sin, however slight; 2) to detach ourselves from every earthly desire; 3) let us not cease our accustomed exercises of prayer and mortification, however great may be the weariness and dryness we feel in them; 4) let us meditate daily on the Passion of Jesus Christ, which inflames with divine love every heart that meditates upon it; 5) let us resign ourselves in peace to the will of God in all things that trouble us; and 6) let us continually beg of God the gift of His holy love....

What do the Saints say that prayer really is?

- "A Manifestation of Divine glory"–St. John of Damascus (690-749)
- "A treasure"–St. Alphonsus Liguori (1686-1787)
- "The Key to Heaven"–St. Augustine (325-430)
- "Man's greatest virtue"–St. Peter Julina Eymard (181-68)
- "A pious way of forcing God"–St. John Climacus (d. 649)
- "The bridge over temptations, and the death of sadness and the token of future glory"–St. John Climacus (d. 649)
- "The holy water that by its glow makes the plants of our good desires grow green and flourish"–St. Francis de Sales (1567-1622)
- "A wine which makes glad the heart of man"–St. Bernard (1090-1153)
- "An importunity which becomes our opportunity"–St. Jerome (342-420)

But along with prayer, the saints never fail to point out the other necessity of sainthood—the Cross and its call to suffering.

Again, St. Thérèsè of Lisieux, who was declared a Doctor of the Church on October 19, 1997, defined this truth in her life as she progressed toward sainthood: "I always understood that to become a saint one had to suffer much." St. John Vianney (1786-1859) echoed this understanding when he said, "I have had crosses in plenty—more than I could carry, almost. I set myself to ask for the love of crosses—then I was happy."

St. John Vianney's words help us to confront the irony of suffering, for what a saint does is not only accept the cross, but ask for it. This is reflected in the questions of St. Teresa of Avila (1515-82): "What did the Lord do to suffer so many trials? Have we read in the lives of the Saints, those who for sure are in heaven, that they had a comfortable life?"

No, we haven't read such teachings. In fact, the truth is that they suffered and even came to cherish suffering. "What I suffered is known only to "One" for whose love and in whose love it is pleasing and glorious to suffer," writes St. Isaac Jogues (1607-46). And, likewise, St. Francis de Sales tells us that "sufferings in themselves are very abhorrent to our inclinations, but when considered, with reference to the will of God, they cause us joy and pleasure."

Indeed, suffering, according to St. Joseph Cofasso (1811-60), has extraordinary merit: "Try to resemble that holy soul who wouldn't give up the least part of her suffering so as not to lose merit thereof." St. Mary Claret agrees, writing that "the temple of the spirit is raised through work and suffering, and I would add that suffering counts for more than work."
But perhaps St. John Bosco's words best define for us why the saints treasure suffering: "Your reward in heaven will make

up completely for all your pain and suffering."

Indeed, the reality of heaven and its great reward again brings us back to the wisdom that drives the saints. They maintain an eye on heaven and their hunger to please God. And they know that God will be hungry to reward them. They also never fail to forget that in their work and their suffering, God will provide the grace they need, especially if they abandon themselves to His Will. For Scripture makes it clear that "God's grace is sufficient" (2 Corinthians 2:9)—always.

"Grace can do nothing without the will," writes St. John Chrysostom, and "will can do nothing without grace." For "if grace is received faithfully," says St. Thérèse of Lisieux, "God will grant a multitude of others."

The saints tell us that there are graces for every area of one's life. But God is especially generous to those souls who "lean on God" and truly desire "holiness." "God is not a deceiver, that He would offer to support us, and then, when we lean upon Him, should slip away from us," St. Augustine (354-430) reassures us. "In sorrow and suffering," St. John of the Cross (1542-91) directs us to "go straight to God with confidence and [we] will be strengthened, enlightened and instructed."

St. John Borromeo explains that this is because "God wishes us not to rest upon anything but His infinite Goodness. Do not let us expect anything, hope anything, but let us put our trust and confidence in him alone."

Perhaps the Savior's own words in Scripture say it best, "Come to me all you that labour and are burdened; I will give you rest. Take my yoke upon yourselves, and learn from Me; I am gentle and humble of heart and you shall find rest for your souls" (Mat 11:28-30).

God will not only give us rest, the saints tell us, but everything we need to become holy; everything we need to become a saint. Perhaps St. Thérèse of Lisieux's words say it all for those who, like her, hunger to be a saint and are not afraid to say so:

> I have always wanted to be a Saint. Alas, I have always noticed that when I compared myself to the Saints, there is between them and me the same difference that exists between a mountain whose summit is lost in the clouds and the obscure grain of sand trampled underfoot by the passer-by. Instead of becoming discouraged, I said to myself, "God cannot inspire unrealizable desires. I can then, in spite of my littleness, aspire to holiness..."

Yes, she did! And so can we!

St. Paul

CHAPTER FOUR

THE FIRST SAINTS

There can be no better way of understanding how and why God will now bring His victory into the world than to understand how God has worked in the past. Since Christ's Ascension, the forces of evil over the last 2000 years have continuously assaulted the Church. The primary goal of this evil, which is demonically inspired and assisted, is to destroy the Catholic Church and the Christian Faith. Indeed, whether through military invasion or internal heresy, Satan's unceasing pressure to destroy souls, ravage the Church, and defeat God is well documented in Scripture. Perhaps St. Paul captured this reality best when he warned the early Church to "put on the armor of God so that you may be able to stand firm against the tactics of the devil. Our battle is not against human forces but against the principalities and powers, the rulers of this world of darkness, the evil spirits in regions above" (Eph 6:11-13).

The spiritual catalyst for much of the evil in the world is unseen, but the perpetrators of this evil are quite often visible. They are the men and women who fail to adhere to St. Paul's advice. They are souls who, because of their sinful state, become seduced into the service of the evil one.

While all men and women are sinners, and certainly evil overwhelms almost everyone at some time in their life, it is no secret that the forces of Hell recruit souls to do their bidding. These are the souls who sin over and above the everyday stumbles and falls caused by submission to temptation. These individuals, the Virgin Mary tells us, embrace sin and then through spiritual blindness begin to champion wrong as right, evil as good. In the very worst cases, these are the faces and figures that history records as tyrants and murderers, enemies of mankind, who bring suffering, division, and death into the world—especially to innocent people.

From Nero to Hitler, many of their names are familiar. But more often than not, many of their names are not known. Nor are the names of their innumerable underlings, who by the millions, have knowingly consented to cooperate in the many grand schemes of evil. They are the ones who on Judgement Day will be seen in their true light, said Christ.

To counter the faces and forces of Satan, there have always been soldiers of God. Like their evil counterparts, some are known but many are not. But through God's grace, the Church is lead to understand that their lives need to be remembered, so their aid can be invoked and their work imitated. For although they are gone, the Church reminds us that they are still with us in many ways, ready to continue the struggle against the legions of Hell.

Thus, as the Church and world now prepare to undergo a climactic struggle that will witness God's greatest victory, let us take a look at some of the historical events and saintly figures of the past who successfully answered the call to defend the Truth of Jesus Christ and His Church. For through their lives and struggles, a panorama of our own times unfolds, giving us a glimpse at what may be expected from the saints of the latter days.

THE EARLY CHURCH

Not long before Christ's Ascension, the Lord told His

Apostles to wait in Jerusalem for the coming of the Holy Spirit. For nine days, the Apostles, the Blessed Virgin Mary, and other disciples of Christ prayed together in what was known as the Upper Room. Suddenly, the sound of a great wind was heard and a ball of fire appeared, dividing into individual flames which hovered over the head of each person in the room. The fire was the visible presence of the Holy Spirit. And in fulfillment of Christ's promise, the Spirit poured out His gifts upon them so that they could truly understand the truths which Christ had given them. The Spirit then fortified them with the courage and love they would need to evangelize the world.

That day is known as Pentecost Sunday, the birthday of the Church, because from that moment the followers of Christ were never again the same. They were transformed from timid, cowardly, uncertain, and confused men into heroic witnesses of Christ. Indeed, that day alone saw, as Scripture tells us, 3,000 converted to the Faith.

After that day, the history of the early Church during the times of the Apostles is seen in the *Acts of the Apostles* and the other Epistles. History tells us that through their words, perseverance, and eventually their blood, the early Church took root and spread. This period primarily confronted the dual challenge of converting the Jews and the pagans of the Hellenistic culture that possessed the Mediterranean at this time. It also confronted the challenge of successfully keeping the early Church alive in the face of its greatest opposition—the Roman Empire.

As we know, the blood of the martyrs flowed freely and often, as the early Christian practice of submitting to persecution was first put to the test. However, within this great story certainly lies many lesser known stories of the great individuals who led the Church down this path.

St. Peter

While Pentecost Sunday was the beginning of the Church, and while all in the Upper Room that day undoubtedly shared in the joys and fruits of that profound experience, one man stood out. St. Peter—who even denied Christ three times—was now to become the strong leader Christ foretold. St. Peter, whose original name was Simon, was a man of weakness and loyalty, whose story illustrates God's way of mysteriously choosing His followers.

A fisherman by trade, he and his brother Andrew, a disciple of John the Baptist, left their nets to follow Christ. Over the next several years, Scripture tells us that Peter witnessed the miracles of Christ and became convinced enough to declare that "He was the Messiah" (Mat 16:16, Lk 9:19). Christ renamed the great Apostle and declared him "Rock," the rock upon which "I will build my Church" (Mat 16:18).

In Scripture we see that St. Peter's role during Christ's life is pivotal and that after the Resurrection he becomes first among all Christ's followers. Throughout the *Acts of the Apostles*, it is St. Peter who is the spokesman for Jesus' followers. He is seen as the great witness of their resurrected faith and his missionary activities take him from Jerusalem to Rome.

It is estimated that St. Peter did not come to Rome before the year 55 A.D. But historians now believe that there is a good chance that St. Peter was executed in Rome on October 13th, 64 A.D. Almost 2,000 years later, St. Peter's bones were identified beneath the main altar in St. Peter's Basilica in Rome. Surely, no one could have known twenty centuries earlier that this very spot would remain the epicenter, the rock, upon which the Catholic Church would be built.

While the heroism of St. Peter is thoroughly documented in

Scripture, his ongoing struggle to serve the Lord faithfully is perhaps seen most clearly in the legendary story known as Quo Vadis.

The story claims that during the Roman persecutions of the Christians in the year 64, Emperor Nero accused the Christians of setting the great fire that destroyed the city in July of that year. St. Peter was persuaded to flee the capital for his own welfare and that of the Christian community. But as he hurried along the Appian Way in the darkness, St. Peter reportedly confronted a familiar man who was walking in the opposite direction back to Rome.

"Where are you going?" inquired Peter of the man. "I am going to Rome to be crucified afresh," the traveler answered. At once, Peter recognized the voice. It was the Lord returning to suffer death again, this time in Rome with His besieged followers. Stricken by conscience, St. Peter is said to have turned back to Rome while the stranger vanished. The next day, Peter was crucified upside down by request, for he felt unworthy to die as his Master had done.

St. Stephen

It would not be possible to understand God's call to suffering without recalling the life and death of St. Stephen. St. Stephen was a learned Greek-speaking Jew who lived in Jerusalem and was converted to Christianity. He was one of the seven chosen by the Twelve to take care of the needs of the Christian community of Jerusalem. He also performed many miracles. But because of his success, some of the elders of the Synagogues in Jerusalem charged him with blasphemy against the Sanhedrin. Before them, he eloquently defended himself and denounced his accusers. Then, as he described a vision of Christ standing at the right hand of the Father, the assembly seized him and dragged him to the outskirts of the city where they stoned him to death. He was the first Christian martyr.

St. Paul

Like St. Peter, St. Paul also saw his name changed from Saul to Paul after his life in Christ took hold. Born of Jewish parents of the tribe of Benjamin, St. Paul originally studied under the famous Jewish rabbi, Gamaliel. A tentmaker by trade, Paul became a strict Pharisee and participated in the persecution of St. Stephen.

On the road to Damascus to continue his persecution of Christians, St. Paul experienced a vision which led to his famous conversion. He then became a great preacher, traveling the world of the Mediterranean to bring the message of the Gospel to the Gentiles.

After being forced to flee secretively, St. Paul spent years teaching and working miracles everywhere from Jerusalem to Spain to Rome. He also wrote many letters, which make up the Epistles to the Romans, Corinthians, Ephesians, Galatians, Colossians, Thessalonians and Philippians. Like St. Peter, he was executed in Rome. However, St. Paul was beheaded and, according to Eusebius (a 4th century priest, lecturer, and canonized saint), his death occurred on the same day as St. Peter (believed to be October 13th) in the year 67 A.D.

The Dispersion of the Apostles

After miraculously escaping King Herod Agrippa's second persecution of the Christians in the year 42 A.D., St. Peter decided it was time for the Apostles to take their mission of spreading the Gospel to all men throughout the known world.

Historians believe that by 42 A.D. all of the Apostles had departed from Jerusalem, except for James the Great, James the Lesser, and St. Peter. Peter soon departed for Rome, while that same year James the Greater was beheaded and James the Lessor became Bishop of Jerusalem.

Traditions tell us that it is believed that St. John and the Virgin Mary traveled to Ephesus in Asia minor. St. Bartholomew went to South Arabia and possibly to India. St. Andrew traveled to the Ukraine and Greece. St. Matthew journeyed to Egypt and Ethiopia. St. Philip also went to Asia Minor. St. Simon traveled to Iran. St. Jude went to Mesopotamia. St. Thomas went to India. Finally, St. Matthias, who was elected to replace Judas, traveled, according to unreliable legend, to Judea, Capodocia, and to the shore of the Caspian Sea.

James the Lessor, after becoming the head of the primitive Church in Jerusalem, is believed to be the same "James" of the *Epistle of James*. He is believed to have wielded authority in making crucial decisions in the early Church. According to Hecesippus, a second century ecclesial historian, James the Lessor was thrown from the pinnacle of the Temple in Jerusalem, and then stoned to death by the Pharisees on May 3, 62 A.D.

Unfortunately, little is known about **Sts. Bartholmew** and **Andrew**. St. Bartholmew, also believed to be Nathaniel of John's Gospel, reportedly was beheaded by King Astyages in Greater Armenia or India. After teaching in Greece and Byzantium, St. Andrew was reportedly crucified , on an X-shaped cross, at Patras Acacia.

James the Greater, the brother of St. John the evangelist, reportedly traveled to Spain where he preached at Zaragosta. He then returned to Jerusalem where he was beheaded by Herod Agrippa I. He was the first Apostle to be martyred.

There is much more evidence concerning the lives of **St. Thomas** and **St. Jude**. It is certain that St. Thomas went by caravan to Taxila in northern India and worked as a carpenter in the Court of Kind Gundofarr. He remained there for several years, winning converts through his preaching. There is also evidence that St. Thomas returned to Jerusalem at the time of the death and Assumption of the Blessed Virgin Mary and to attend the Council of Jerusalem. He then returned to India in the year 52 A.D. He reportedly arrived at Malabar on the southwestern coast of India, where tradition says he cured hundreds and baptized thousands.

After seventeen years, St. Thomas then traveled to Mylapore, near the city of Madias on the opposite coast. It was there one day in 72 A.D. that St. Thomas was praying in a cave and was attacked by priests from the Temple of Kali, the Indian goddess of death. He reportedly died from a lance that pierced his heart. He was buried in Mylapore where the Christian community he founded survived for over a thousand years.

The account of the life of the Apostle St. Jude is connected with the history of the Church's most important relic, the Holy Shroud (also known as the Shroud of Turin). Responding to leprosy-stricken King Abgar of northwestern Mesopotamia, the Apostle Jude was sent with the Holy Shroud. King Abgar requested that Christ come to cure him, but Christ had already ascended. Believed to be perhaps the first Apostolic mission, St. Jude brought the Shroud to Edessa where King Abgar was cured and then baptized into the Church. St. Jude went on to preach in Mesopotamia and was later martyred in Persia on October 28th.

St. Simon, known as the Zealot, is said to have been a preacher in Mauretania, then in Africa, and finally in Britain. Several different sources support Simon's visit to Britain and then, around the year 66, he teamed up with St. Jude where together they met their demise in Iran.

St. Matthew, because of his Gospel, is generally considered to be well known, but is actually one of the Apostles that least is known about after Christ's death. He is, however, almost indisputably credited with the authorship of his Gospel, which is believed to have been written between 50 A.D. and 70 A.D. in Jerusalem. St. Matthew is also known to have ministered to the Jewish community in Palestine for fifteen years. Some records place him in Ethiopia for as long as twenty-three years. Here he is said to have performed miracles and even "raised the dead." According to the history of Abcias, St. Matthew was martyred in Ethiopia. But other accounts have him living to an old age in Persia and dying of natural causes.

St. Matthias, who replaced Judas, reportedly lived a life of great austerity. Supposedly, his precept was that one should "treat the flesh with contempt." He is said to have taught converts that they must "renounce desire" and that they "could not serve two masters—"pleasure and the lord." St. Matthias is described in tradition as having traveled to Armenia. There, he reportedly assisted St. Andrew. In or around the year 51. A.D., he reportedly returned to Jerusalem where tradition has it he was stoned to death by a crowd of hostile Jews. He was the second of the twelve to die.

St. Philip was believed to have originally been a disciple of St. John the Baptist. He was called by Jesus Himself (Jn1:43-48) and brought Nathaniel to Christ. According to tradition, he preached in Greece and was crucified upside down at Hieraopolis under Emperor Domitian.

Finally, **St. John the Evangelist**, who was the only Apostle at the Crucifixion, is believed to have lived a long life and was perhaps the only Apostle spared martyrdom. Scripture

45

says that he was imprisoned with St. Peter and appeared with him before the Sanhedrin (Acts 4-12). He accompanied St. Peter to Samaria (Acts 8:14) to transmit the Holy Spirit to the new converts, and attended the Council of Jerusalem in 49 A.D. After this, he traveled to Asia Minor and is believed to have been with the Virgin Mary until the Assumption. He is named by St. Paul, along with St. Peter and St. James, as "these leaders, these pillars" of the Church in Jerusalem (Gal 2:9).

According to tradition, St. John journeyed to Rome during the reign of Domitian where he miraculously escaped from a cauldron of boiling oil and was exiled to the island of Patmos. There he wrote the *Book of Revelation*. After the death of Domitian in 96 A.D., he returned to Ephesus where he wrote the fourth Gospel and three Epistles. He is believed to have died in 104 A.D.

Several other prominent Saints of this period must be cited. **St. Mark**, who authored one of the Gospels, is credited with founding the Church of Alexandria in Egypt. He was a Levite who accompanied St. Paul and **St. Barnabas** to Antioch in 44 A.D., then to Cyprus, and along with St. Barnabas was on St. Paul's first missionary journey. He evidently became a disciple of St. Peter, who referred to him as "my son" (1 Pet 5:13). His Gospel was probably written in Rome between 60 and 70 A.D. for gentile Christians.

St. Luke, the evangelist and also the author of the third gospel, preached in different parts of Achaea. He accompanied St. Paul and was a physician. After St. Paul's death, he went to Greece. It is believed that he wrote his Gospel between the years 70 and 90 A.D. He is also credited with writing Acts, probably in Rome after St. Paul's death. He suffered martyrdom in Thebes.

Replacing St. Barnabas, **St. Timothy** joined St. Paul at Lysta and became St. Paul's close friend and confidant. St. Paul allowed him to be circumcised in order to placate the Jews, since he was the son of a Jew.

St. Timothy accompanied St. Paul on his second missionary journey and remained in Berea when St. Paul was forced to flee because of the Jews there. He was probably with St. Paul when the Apostle was imprisoned at Caesarea and then Rome, and was himself imprisoned, but set free.

According to tradition, he became the first Bishop of Ephesus, where he was then stoned to death when he opposed a pagan festival of Katacogian in honor of the goddess Diana. St. Paul wrote two letters to St. Timothy while he awaited execution—one about 65 A.D. and the second from Rome while he awaited execution. St. Timothy died in 97 A.D.

St. John the Evangelist

CHAPTER FIVE

THE AGE OF MARTYRS

The rise of Christianity in the world is certainly one of the greatest stories of all time. It is a story of drama and persevering success. It highlights the role of hope in our lives, and—while Jesus Christ, true God and true man, is the focus of the story—it has more heroes than perhaps any other human struggle in history.

The sagas of SS. Peter and Paul and the early disciples of Christ are deserving legends, but this story in many ways, only gets better. For some reason, almost every conceivable trial and tribulation arises with the spread of Christianity, and God, therefore, presents generous opportunities for the rise of new and equally exciting heroes. These memorable and timeless characters emerge on the world stage victorious— regardless if they live or die. For the Church, as God promises, can never die.

With the deaths of SS. Peter and Paul and the Apostles came the end of the beginning. Christ's words—proclaiming that the Kingdom of God was at hand—indicated the beginning of the end. The Church was established. It was not going away. And most of all, it had a world wide mission to accomplish.

Not long after the deaths of SS. Peter and Paul, a landmark event occurred which Christ foretold. Jerusalem fell to the Romans in a bloody clash, and the Temple in Jerusalem went up in flames. Indeed, "not one stone" was left upon another, as Christ had prophesied.

This extraordinary event is perhaps underestimated by most, but according to historians, it was, in reality, "one of the most memorable and important events in the history of mankind." Indeed, while over a million Jews died and 97,000 were sold into slavery, the overall impact of this event on the future of the world is perhaps inestimable. This is because both Christianity and Judaism were profoundly affected. Survivors were dispersed or forced to disperse to every quarter of the known world.

Almost fifty years after the fall of Jerusalem, a final uprising and defeat of the Jews completed this dispersal. This also completed the shift in the times, for now the world would slowly be molded and reshaped by the emerging force of Christianity. Indeed, it is ironic that the Jews of our time still refuse to see what happened to them with the crucifixion of Christ. For the most part, three major events took place shortly after the death of Christ which support this shift: (1) the destruction of the Temple, (2) the ending of animal sacrifices, and (3) the dispersal of the tribe of Judah.

While Rome would still rule for the next four centuries, the internal metamorphosis of its culture from that of paganism to Christianity had also begun. The seeds had been planted by the Apostles, and now all that was needed was for the Church to take root. In the caves of Palestine and the catacombs of Rome, this stage of growth took place. And as history records very clearly, it was a growth that was nourished by the blood of its witnesses.

While there are many reasons given for the advancement of early Christianity, the primary cause of the rapid spread of the Christian faith was the divine assistance that Christ had promised: "Behold I am with you all days even to the consummation of the world" (Mat 28:20). Like the Apostles and early disciples, numerous miracles accompanied the preaching of the Gospel. But since this power was given—not for the sake of believers, as St. Paul clarifies, but for the sake of unbelievers—miracles eventually became less frequent, though they never completely ceased.

The zeal of converts certainly emerged in the early Church to be just as important as miracles in the spread of Christianity. Most importantly, this zeal was demonstrated by how often the Christians were ready to lay down their lives for their Faith.

If we are to understand what caused these saints to do what they did, we must grasp what historians tell us about their belief system. They were convinced that Christianity was not one belief system among many. Rather, they believed it was the one, true, revealed religion of the one, true, revealed God—a religion to which the entire world must be converted. Historians say that the driving force of such an uncompromising attitude was the complete trust that Christianity was the absolute Truth. These convictions inspired great enthusiasm and heroism, catapulting the faith forward despite the danger of the times.

Each day was a significant step towards the Church's eventual triumph over the Roman empire. History marks the names of some of the men and women involved in this effort, especially the martyrs who, at particularly crucial moments, guided the Church safely through the storms of the first several centuries. We, the children of the martyrs, should regard the deeds of these early Christians with great reverence—perhaps as much we do those of the Apostles and early disciples.

"I have often sat before the *Acts of the Martyrs* with tears in my eyes," writes the eminent historian Adam Moehler, "sympathizing within their sufferings, marveling at their deeds, moved to the depths of my soul by their heroism. If we can ever be so ungrateful as to forget the martyrs, we deserve to be forgotten by Christ the Savior."

Both in the holy land and in Rome, the 2nd century saw these heroes step forward in faith. **St. Simeon**, who succeeded St. James in the See of Jerusalem, was one of the first victims. He was condemned to die on the cross. Another great saint of the First Century was St. Ignatius of Antioch. In the year 107, St. Ignatius, a disciple of the Apostles, was thrown to the lions in the theater at Rome. He had become the Bishop of Antioch and was known for his hatred of heresy and schism and his ardent desire for martyrdom. Most significantly, St. Ignatius was the first to use the term "Catholic Church." He also lead the defense of the Church against one of the very first heresies—Docetism, which denied the humanity of Christ and ascribed to Him a phantom body.

During the reign of Trajan, **St. Clement**—the third successor of St. Peter in Rome—and many other Christians suffered death. In Asia Minor, around the year 112, a considerate number of Christians were martyred in Bithynia.

Probably the most heralded saint to be martyred in the 2nd century was **St. Polycarp**. St. Polycarp was the aged bishop of Smyrna and for nearly thirty years was a disciple and companion of the Apostle and evangelist St. John. St. Irenaeus (125-203), who was a pupil of Polycarp, recorded a detailed account of his memories:

> I remember the events of that time more clearly than those of recent occurrence. The lessons of childhood grow with the growth of

the soul, and become one with it. And so I can describe the very place in which the blessed Polycarp used to sit as he discoursed, and his going out and his comings in , and his manner of life, and his personal appearance, and the discourses which he made to the people, and how he would describe his intercourse with John and the rest who had seen the Lord, and how he would relate their words. And whatsoever things he had heard from them about the Lord, and about His miracles, and about His teachings, Polycarp, as having received them from eyewitnesses of the life of the Word, would relate all in keeping with the Scriptures.

At the age of 86, St. Polycarp was arrested and brought before the Roman procounsel and a stadium full of onlookers. Repeatedly refusing to deny Christ, St. Polycarp was finally ordered to be burned at the stake.

Another great saint of the 2nd century was **St. Justin**. Again, his sacrifice was made as a direct rebuke to Roman tyranny, which was attempting to destroy the Christian Faith. St. Justin was especially hated because his writings eloquently defended the Faith against not only the leaders of Rome, but also the Jews. After spending many years in Rome, he then traveled to the Holy Land. In Bethlehem, he spent many years translating Scripture into Latin. This eventually became the official Scriptural text of the Church.

In the reign of Marcus Aurelius (161-180), St. Justin and six other Christians were accused before the prefect of Rome of refusing to sacrifice to the gods. They were then beheaded. An eye witness record of the trial survives to this day:

The Prefect (to St. Justin): 'Hearken, you who are called learned and think that you know the truth: if you are scourged and beheaded, do you believe that you will ascend into heaven?'

St. Justin: 'I hope that if I endure these things I shall have this privilege, for I know that to all who have thus lived there abides the divine favor until the consummation of the world.'

The Prefect: 'Do you suppose that you will ascend into heaven to receive such a recompense?'

St. Justin: 'No one who is in his right senses will pass from piety to impiety.'

The Prefect: 'If you do not obey, you will be punished unmercifully.'

St. Justin: 'It is our heart's desire to be martyred for our Lord Jesus Christ and then to be happy forever.'

Thus also said the other Christians, 'Do what you will, for we are Christians and do not sacrifice to idols.'

Thereupon the Prefect pronounced sentence saying, 'Let those who have refused to sacrifice to the gods and to obey the command of the Emperor be scourged and led away to suffer decapitation according to the law.'

The holy martyrs having glorified God and having gone forth to the accustomed place, were beheaded, and perfected their testimony in the confession of the

Savior. And some of the faithful, having secretly removed their bodies, laid them in a suitable place.

In Gaul (France), another horrific massacre of Christians occurred around the year 177. Again, refusing to deny their faith, these Christians were tortured inhumanly and then lead to their death. Some were devoured by wild beasts in the amphitheaters, others were killed in prison. Two saints, **St. Pothinus**, the 90 year old Bishop of the city, and **St. Blandina**, a young slave girl, are especially remembered. St. Blandina reportedly endured so many different kinds of torment, that each one should have killed her. Instead, she reportedly kept repeating, "I am Christian," which caused her to be invigorated with fresh strength. Finally, she was gored by a bull and trampled to death.

One of the great theologians and saints of the beginning the 3rd century was **St. Irenaeus**. He was a theologian and great defender of the Church against heresies. As noted, St. Irenaeus was a disciple of St. Polycarp. He defended the Church against Gnosticism, which held that there was one supreme spirit who was incomprehensible and entirely removed from the world. St. Irenaeus's writings, which included *Against the Heresies* and *The Proof of the Apostolic Teaching* are considered of inestimable value in the history of the early Church. He was martyred in the year 202.

Many more heroic accounts of the 3rd century are recorded. The martyrs of Scilla, outside Carthage in North Africa, feature the heroic story of **St. Cecelia**, a noble Roman lady, who chose to remain "undefiled" on her wedding day. Likewise, from Egypt, comes the Story of **St. Leonidas**, the father of the great Origen. Origen, but a child, extolled his father to seize the martyr's crown along with multitudes of other Christians in Egypt. St. Leonidas and his friends were cast into prison, torn with iron hooks, devoured by wild and exotic beasts, burned, beheaded, and crucified.

While there are countless stories of the early martyrs and the birth pangs of the Church as it emerged throughout the Roman empire, perhaps the story of St. Perpetua serves as a representative narrative of this period of Church history.

SS. Perpetua and **Felecitas** and their companions suffered martyrdom at Carthage on the 7th of March in the year 203. St. Perpetua, a young wife and mother, wrote of her experiences from the time she was arrested until she was martyred. They were later rewritten in story form and included in the *Age of the Martyrs:*

> It had come to the ears of the authorities that the noble lady Perpetua, contrary to the edict of Septimius Severus, was receiving instruction in the Christian religion with several members of her household, among them her brother Saturus and the slaves Felicitas and Rovocatus. Armed soldiers entered her house and arrested all who professed themselves as Christians.
>
> 'When I was in the hands of the persecutors,' she writes 'my father, who was an obstinate pagan, in his tender solicitude tried hard to pervert me from the faith.'
>
> 'Father,' I said, 'you see this pitcher. Can we call it by any other name than what it is? Neither can I call myself by any other name than that of Christian.'
> So he went away, but, on the rumor that we

were to be tried, wasted away with anxiety, he returned.

'Daughter,' he said, 'have pity on my gray hairs; have pity on thy father. Do not give me over to disgrace. Behold thy brother, thy mother, and thy aunt: behold thy child, who cannot live without thee. Do not destroy us all.'

Thus spake my father, kissing my hands, and throwing himself at my feet. And I wept because of my father, for he alone of all my family would not rejoice in my martyrdom. So I comforted him, saying:
'In this trial, what God determines will take place. We are not in our own keeping, but God's. So he left me, weeping bitterly.'

Perpetua was allowed to keep her little boy with her in prison, and she nursed him with such motherly tenderness and such resignation to God's will that the captain of the prison guard was moved to pity and made her prison days as pleasant as possible for her.

Three days before the time set for the execution, Felicitas gave birth to a child. She suffered intense pain, which she could not hide from the rude soldiers on guard.

'If you lament and cry out now,' one of them said to her, 'what will you do when you are thrown to the wild beasts?'

'I am suffering alone,' she replied, 'what I am suffering now; then, Another will be with me, who will suffer for me, because I will suffer for Him.'

The dreadful day arrived. The little band of Christians was led into the arena, Perpetua singing a hymn, and the men proclaiming aloud to all the spectators the coming judgement of God. First they were scourged; then leopards, bears and wild boars were let loose upon the men. Perpetua and Felicitas were tossed and gored by a mad cow; but in spite of cruel mangling, yet survived. Perpetua seemed in a trance. "When are we going to be tossed?" she asked, and could scarcely believe that she had suffered, until she saw the ugly gash in her thigh. Presently all were stabbed to death. Perpetua had to guide to her own throat the unsteady hand of the young gladiator. The noble woman Perpetua and the slave woman Felicitas are commemorated together in the Canon of the Mass. Their feast is celebrated on the 6th of March.

The Roman persecutions continued until the year 312. After Emperor Constantine obtained a victory attributed to a vision and dream directing him to fight under the "sign of the Christian cross," he finally issued the Edict of Milan. This order allowed for anyone, "including the Christians—[to] observe the faith of this...cult." With this, the Roman empire was now officially neutral toward religion.

Not long after this, a string of great heresies besieged the Church. These new conflicts again precipitated the rise of many great saints who were willing, ready, and able to defend Christ's Church.

St. Augustine

CHAPTER SIX

THE ARIAN CONTROVERSY

With the official acceptance of Christianity by the Roman empire, it wasn't long before the Church was under attack from a new enemy, the enemy within its own ranks.

During the 3rd, 4th, and 5th centuries, a series of events occurred within the Church that threatened its very foundation. Coming at a time when communication was poor, keeping the Church united in truth proved to be a difficult task. New interpretations of who Christ really was, what exactly constituted His complete nature, and who possessed the authority to define the truth were all major issues of the times. These issues and more created division. This, as Christ Himself warned, posed great danger to the survival of the true Church.

More often than not, the heresies that arose were almost logical in nature. The truth that Jesus Christ was truly the Son of God, the Messiah foretold to come by the Jewish prophets, was difficult for many to understand and accept. It confronted existing teachings in a very direct manner, causing people to fear that if they were making a mistake, they would offend their god or gods.

Of course, the Holy Spirit was at work to help illuminate the truth, but the religion of Christianity at that time was only beginning to be defended with authority. Significant questions were posed. And these questions, many of a doctrinal nature, needed to be intellectually challenged for the good of the Church. Indeed, as history shows, a good debate over questionable issues only results in the truth becoming clearer and better defined.

The first great heresy was Arianism, named after a man named Arius. Arius believed and taught that since Christ was the Son of God, a father must precede a son. Therefore, Christ could not be divine, but must be a created creature of God. The forerunner of this school of thought was actively seen in the last decade of the second century. A man named Theodoctus was excommunicated by Pope St. Victor for declaring that Christ was a mere man. But this set off many questions, especially whether or not Christ was God, as the Father was God. And was He eternal? And equal in power and glory? Several other forerunners to Arianism arose, but because Arius himself was an esteemed and charismatic figure, this local affair soon spread throughout the whole empire.

Now God again was prepared to come to the rescue of His Church. As He had through the inspiring heroism of the martyrs—which ironically caused the Church to thrive not die—the Lord moved His chosen servants in a special way to again bring about a victory.

First, an Ecumenical Council was held at Nicea on May 20, 325. Approximately 318 bishops attended and produced historical results. The Council determined that a condemnation of Arianism was not only warranted, but it was necessary. A clear statement defining the Catholic faith was needed—a statement that definitively established the Divinity of Jesus Christ. This lead to the Nicene Creed.

Although Arianism was condemned, it continued to be practiced by many Christians. In response to this emerged a great defender of faith, a man named Athanasius. **St. Athanasius**, while little known, is perhaps one of the greatest saints in Church history. Considered by some to be the "outstanding personality in the Roman world," St. Athanasius withstood threats, exile, ridiculous charges, and seductive promises in his vigilant battle against Arianism (see St. Athanasius under "The Great Saints").

This period of the Arian heresy saw the rise of other great saints of the "Nicene faith." In the east, came the "Three Cappadocians"—St. Basil the Great, St Gregory of Nazanius, and St. Gregory of Nyssa.

St. Basil assisted in combating Arianism and became an archbishop. He was a leader of orthodoxy and denounced Arianism at the Council of Constantinople in 381-382. He also fought Simony, aided the poor and victims of drought and famine, strove to improve the clergy, and denounced evil wherever he detected it. He was a statesman, a man of great personal holiness, and a great orator. In addition to his letters and books, he was also recognized for an outstanding treatise on the Holy Spirit. He is a Doctor of the Church.

St. Gregory of Nazanius was a friend of St. Basil and another heroic figure in the Arian controversy. His exceptional preaching brought about numerous conversions, as it did alarm and persecutions from the Arians. He was eventually named Archbishop of Constantinople. Like St. Basil, he is also a Doctor of the Church and is often surnamed "the Theologian" for his eloquent defense of the faith and the decrees of the Nicene Creed in his sermons and Treatises.

St. Gregory of Nyssa was also a major figure in the Asian controversy. He was formerly a professor of Rhetoric who suffered exile and imprisonment because of the Arian controversy. Like St. Basil and Gregory of Nazianius, he wrote brilliantly and was called "Father of the Fathers" by the Second General Council of Nicea.

The final victory of Catholicism over Arianism is generally recognized with an edict that was declared on February 28, 380. This abolished Arianism and marked the complete reunion of the East and the West, which had been separated during this century. This edict, issued by Gratian and Theodosius, was no simple statement, for it declared that those who still advocated the teachings of Arius were mad, insane, and deserving of Divine vengeance:

> We will that all peoples who are ruled by the authority of our clemency shall hold to the religion which the Divine Apostle Peter delivered to the Romans, and which is recognized by his having preserved it there until the present day, and which it is known that the Pontiff Damasus follows, and Peter, Bishop of Alexandria, a man of apostolic holiness, that is to say, that according to the teaching of the Apostles and the doctrine of the Gospel, we should believe in one Godhead of the Father, Son, and Holy Ghost, in co-equal majesty and Holy Trinity. We order those who follow this law to take the name of Catholic Christians; all others, mad and insane, we condemn to the infamy of heresy, and they will be punished in the first place by divine vengeance, and also by penalties, wherein we follow the will of Heaven.

CHAPTER SEVEN

THE LAST DAYS

During the 4th and 5th centuries, more great saints and defenders of the faith arose. **St. Jerome** (342-420), a great scholar of Latin, Greek, and classic authors, denounced the Meletian-schism controversy and went on to study Scripture under St. Gregory the Nanzianzen. In 382, St. Jerome went to Rome where he remained a secretary to Pope Damasus. While there, he revised the Latin version of the four Gospels, St. Paul's Epistles, and the Psalms. He wrote *Adversum Helvidium*, which denounced a book by Helvidius declaring that Mary had several children.

With the death of Pope Damascus, St. Jerome traveled east in 385. He continued to write in defense of the faith and his greatest achievement was his translation of the Old Testament from Hebrew into Latin. This version, called the Vulgate, was declared the official Scriptural text of the Church by the Council of Trent and was used up until the middle of the 20th century. Pope John Paul II replaced it with a new vulgate in 1979. St. Jerome was deservedly declared a Doctor of the Church.

St. John Chrystostom (347-402) was such a great orator of the faith that his sermons earned him the title "golden-mouthed." He abandoned the forum, the theater, and the halls of learning at a very young age to devote himself exclusively to prayer and study of the Scriptures. For years he lived with monks on a mountain; for two years he lived alone in a cave. He would sleep without lying down, expose himself to extreme cold, and endure other self-induced sufferings to make up for his pleasure-filled life as a youth.

After becoming a priest he wrote and lectured for ten years, establishing himself as a great pulpit orator. Caught up in the controversies of his times, he eventually was banished to Pityus on the northeast coast of the Black Sea. He died, however, in route. The Church recognizes him as the "last and greatest of the Eastern Fathers." He is, according to some, "the supreme effort and last splendor of Christian genius in the east."

St. Augustine (354-430) began his great career by trying, after reading Cicero, to conquer his own immortality through "the acquisition of true wisdom." "Every vain hope" writes Augustine, "at once became worthless to me and I longed with incredibly burning desire for an immortality of wisdom, and I began now to arise, that I might return to thee." In pursuit of this desire, Augustine held an oriental seat of learning for nine years, which ultimately resulted in his opposition to Catholicism.

But his mother, **St. Monica**, horrified at Augustine's atheistic views, persevered in prayer for her son's conversion.

As time passed, the study of Plato led Augustine to God, but he still knew something was missing in philosophy. He was then lead to St. Ambrose, who brought him to Christ and the Church. St. Augustine went from Plato to St. Paul, but though intellectually convinced, he could not make the ultimate sacrifice of renouncing his ambitions and sensual joys. His soul, he would later write, "was on the rack" torn between "the spirit and the flesh."

Eventually, St. Augustine resolved his spiritual conflicts. In his book, *Church History,* Fr. John Laux describes this conversion:

Someone read to him the *Life of St. Antony*, by St. Athanasius and it marked a crisis in his life. 'I saw' he says, 'how foul I was, how distorted and filthy, how soiled and ulcered. And I saw, and shuddered, and could not flee from myself . . . . The day had come when I lay naked to myself.' Then he hears of the sudden conversion of two Roman officers, who had abandoned their military careers and embraced the monastic life. The effect produced in him was nothing short of miraculous. 'What ails us?' he cried out to his friend Alypius. 'The unlearned start up and take heaven by violence, while we with all our learning, all our want of heart, see where we wallow in flesh and blood!' He could no longer bear to be inside the house; in terrible excitement he rushed into the garden, Alyeius, marveling and terrified, at his side, and sat for a while in bitter mediation on the impotence and slavery of the human will. 'The empty trifles, and the vanities of vanities, my loves of old, still held me back, plucking softly at my robe of flesh, and softly whispering,"Wilt though dismiss us? And from this moment shall not this and that be allowed to thee any more forever? Thinkest thou to do without these things?"' On the other side there arose up before him the army of the pure, youths and maidens, men and women, and Chastity herself in all her serene cheerful majesty, who seemed to mock him with the words,`Canst not thou do what these have done, these boys and girls? ' He tore himself from Alypius, ran to the farthest part of the garden, flung himself under a fig-tree, and wept and poured out his heart to God. Suddenly he heard the voice of a child singing from a house near-by some trifling song with the refrain: `Take up and read! Take up and read!' He left off weeping, returned to Alypius, opened the volume of St. Paul's Epistles at random and read in silence the following: 'Not in riotings and drunkenness, not in chamberings and impurities, not in contention and envy, but put ye on the Lord Jesus Christ and make not provisions for the flesh and its lusts' (Rom 13:13-14).

'I had neither desire nor need to read farther,' he says. 'The miracle of grace was worked in calm and silence.' He went straight to his mother and told her what had happened. 'She leaped for joy and triumphed and blessed Thee, Who art able to do above that which we ask or think; for Thou hast given her more for me, than she was wont to beg by her pitiful and most sorrowful groanings.'

After accepting baptism, St. Augustine went on to be a priest. His writings *City of God* and *Confessions* are Catholic Classics. And according to Father Laux, his "Ninth Book" in *Confessions* is a soaring accomplishment:

We said: If the tumult of the flesh were hushed, hushed the images of earth, and waters, and air, hushed also the poles of heaven, yea if the very soul were hushed to herself, hushed of all dreams and fantasies, every tongue and every sigh, and whosoever comes and goes and we could but hear their last word: 'We made not ourselves, but He made us that abideth forever'; if they too should then be hushed, and He alone spoke, not by them, but by Himself that we may hear His word not through any tongue of flesh nor Angel's voice nor sound of thunder, not in the dark riddle of a similitude, but might hear Him whom in these things we love, might hear His very self without these, could this be continued on and on, and all other visions be withdrawn and the one alone ravish and absorb and wrap up its beholder and plunge him into the innermost depths of joy, so that life might be forever like that one moment of understanding when we two strained ourselves and in swift thought touched on the Eternal Truth, and which now we sighed after, would not this`Enter into thy Master's joy'?

Monica died peacefully a few days later. Her last request was for a daily memento at the altar "from which she knew that holy Sacrifice to be dispensed, by which the hand-writing that was against us is blotted out." Augustine concludes his own prayer for his mother by asking his readers to remember her too at the altar, "that so her last request of me may be more fully granted through the prayers of many than through my own poor prayers."

St. Augustine spent thirty-five years as a bishop and took a leading part in the activities of the Church in Africa and all of Christendom. And, like so many of the great figures of the times, he found himself involved in the great heresies of the age, first the Manichaeans, the Donatisits, and then the Pelegreams.

The Donatists maintained that the validity of the Sacraments depended on the moral character of the minister. The Pelagranists believed man could merit the Beatific Vision by His natural powers. They used such Christian terms as baptism, grace, original sin, and redemption, but attached completely new definitions to them. St. Augustine turned his pen on them and issued a series of writings which led to the demise of both heresies. However, according to Father Laux, it is St. Augustine's *City of God* that is the most grandiose defense for Christianity every written:

> On August 24, 410, Rome was taken and pillaged by the Visigoths under Alaric. The pagans laid the blame for this catastrophe on Christianity. Century after century, they said the ancient god of Rome had been victorious; one century of Christianity had sufficed to bring ruin on the Eternal City. These reproaches and blasphemies, says St. Augustine, 'set my heart on fire with zeal for the house of God, and I commenced to write the books of the City of God against the blasphemies and errors of the pagans. This work occupied me for a number of years owing to numerous interruptions of businesses that would not brook delay and had a prior claim on me. At last this large work was brought to a conclusion in twenty-two books.'
> The first part of the *City of God* is the most grandiose defense of Christianity against paganism every written. In the second part (Books 11 to 22) he deals with the history of the *City of Man*, founded upon love of self, and of the *City of God*, founded upon love of God and contempt of self. Through all the

ages these two cities move side by side, each
to its destiny. Christianity is the key to the
world's history. It is the divine light that
illuminates and explains the story of
humanity.

Finally, there remains one more immortal Father of the
Church that must be remembered. **St. Ambrose** of Milan,
Augustine's teacher, grew up during the Arian heresy. He
became a lawyer and was appointed governor of the province
of Milan. But one day while seeking to quell a dispute over
who was to be the next bishop, a child interrupted his speech
by remarking "Ambrose Bishop." The cry raced through the
hall, and Ambrose, not yet even baptized, joined the faith and
was consecrated bishop. St. Ambrose became an active
bishop who struggled against paganism. Indeed, history
records that in a fierce debate before the Emperor in 384, St.
Ambrose "carried the day" and "paganism went into a final,
fatal decline."

Next, Ambrose engaged St. Augustine, who at the time was
an agent of the Manicheans. In fact, it was St. Ambrose who
baptized St. Augustine. But it was St. Ambrose's
confrontation with the emperor Theodosius that lead to a clear
confrontation between the Church and the State. Of course,
St. Ambrose prevailed, making it clear that even Caesar must
render to God the things that are of God. His reverence for
the Holy See is summarized in the famous expression:
"Where there is Peter, there is the Church."

Though the 5th and 6th centuries saw the Church spread its
wings and solidly define its doctrines, it was plagued by new
heresies. And, therefore, more saints were needed to defend
the Church.

The Nestorian heresy is named after a monk of Antioch who preached that Christ was no God, but rather a man whom God dwelt in as a temple. Christ, said Nestorius, became God "by degrees." He also denied that Mary was the mother of God.

St. Cyril, patriarch of Alexandria, refuted the sermons of Nestorius. And Pope Celestine I upheld him. On June 22, 431, a Council was held in Ephesus, where the writings of Nestorius were unanimously condemned. Nestorius, who refused to attend, was then excommunicated. That night, the people of Ephesus rejoiced with a torchlight procession and proclaimed Mary as "Theotokas! Theotokas!"

At the same time, an opposing heresy emerged. This heresy, known as Monophysitism, denied that Christ had a human nature. Monophysitists argued that Christ possessed only a Divine nature because His human nature "was absorbed in His Divinity, like a drop of wine in an ocean."

Monophysitism was so diametrically opposed to Catholic doctrine on the Redemption that Flavian, the Patriarch of Constantinople, immediately deposed and excommunicated Eutyches, its founder. Again a council was formed at Ephesus on August 8, 449. However, the synod acquitted Eutyches and deposed Flavian, who died while returning to Constantinople. **Pope Leo the Great** (440-461) called the Synod, the "Robber Synod" and called a new council. The new council of Chalcedon, upon hearing Pope Leo's Dogmatic Epistle, rose unanimously and exclaimed, "That is the faith of the Fathers, that is the faith of the Apostles, so we all believe! Peter has spoken through Leo."

However, the definition of the Council of Chalcedon, was not embraced by the whole Church. To this day, the remains of the Monophysit controversy exist in schisms in Egypt, Syria, and other countries where Greek was not the official language.

Ironically, the last effort to conciliate the Monophsites in the 7th century actually resulted in another heresy known as the Monotheisis Heresy. This heresy tried to proclaim that there was only one will in Christ. However, this heresy was denounced as nothing but a "disguised Monophysism" and was finally condemned by the Sixth General Council at Constantinople in 680.

The entire era is understood to have ended with a series of invasions from the uncivilized barbarian tribes of central Asia and eastern Asia. Finally in 452, a great hoard of Huns, lead by Attila the Great, advanced toward Rome for a final attack on the city. Heroic defense of the Faith is captured in a story about this confrontation. Fr. John Laux offers this account:

> In the spring of 452 Attila had recovered sufficiently from the effects of his defeat in the Catalaunian Plains to invade Italy. He took and destroyed Aquileia, burned the cities at the head of the Adriatic, plundered Milan and Padua, and prepared to descend upon Rome. The Romans, unable to offer effective resistance, resolved to sue for peace.

Prosper of Aquitaine (400-63), a 5th century historian provides us with the outcome of this confrontation:

> The most blessed Pope Leo, trusting in the help of God who never deserts His friends, took this difficult enterprise upon himself He was accompanied only by the ex-consul Avienus and the ex-Prefect Trygetius. His confidence in God was rewarded; for the deputation was respectfully received, and the king (Attila) was so well pleased with the presence of the Sovereign Pontiff that he gave

orders to cease from war, promised to make
peace, and withdrew beyond the Danube.

In time, the drama of this event was enhanced and
immortalized in Raphael's painting, *Stanza d'Eliodor*. The
legend is told by Paul the Deacon, the Lombard historian (c.
750), in his *Historia Romana* (XIV, 12,2):

> After the departure of the Pontiff, Attila was
> asked by his followers why he had, contrary to
> his custom shown so much reverence to the
> Roman Pope and acceded to his every
> demand; the king replied, 'I did not fear the
> person of him who came to me, but at his side
> I saw another man, clothed in sacerdotal
> vestments, of imposing stature and venerable
> age, who with drawn sword menaced me with
> death unless I agreed to carry out all that was
> demanded of me.'

A still later legend associated St. Paul with St. Peter in the
apparition. In St. Leo's letter to Bishop Julian of Kios he
speaks of the deliverance from the "scourge as a special gift
of the Divine Mercy."

CHAPTER EIGHT

THE CHRISTIANIZATION OF THE BARBARIANS

After the fall of the Western Empire in Europe, the Church—conscious of her eternal message—set out to civilize and Christianize the barbarians. Again, great saints lighted the way with their heroic missionary efforts. The Goths, the Vandals, the Lombards, and the Bergundians were converted to Christianity in the 4th century through the efforts of Theophilus, one of the Nicene Fathers, and Wulfila, who had been captured by the Goths. Wulfila translated the bible into the Gothic language.

In 493, Frankish King Clovis married Chotilda, a Bergundian princess who was a devout Catholic. This led to the conversion of the Franks. The conversion of Ireland also took place during this period. In 432, **St. Patrick** returned to Ireland where he had been held captive, and set about to convert the pagan Druids. He established monasteries and especially worked to convert the kings and chieftains of the island. He knew that this was the fastest way to convert all of Ireland to the Faith.

Around the same time, another significant effort on behalf of the Church was underway. **St. Benedict**, who was born about 480, sought the monastic life but soon became a prophet and a miracle worker. Fr. John Laux writes that St. Benedict went on to found monasteries and his Rule became a code of conduct used for centuries:

> The Benedictine Rule is not only the work of a man of great prudence and moderation; its author was also possessed of an extraordinary talent for organization. Its eminently practical statues could be applied to any association of monks. It is a masterpiece of spiritual legislation, and those who lived up to its letter and its spirit could not but become perfect Christians. And that was the purpose St. Benedict had in view. 'Let the monks,' he says, 'mutually surpass each other in reverence. Let them most patiently tolerate their weaknesses, whether of body or character; let them vie with each other in showing obedience. Let no one pursue what he thinks useful for himself, but rather what he thinks useful for another. Let them love their abbot with a sincere and humble love; let them prefer nothing whatever to Christ who leads us alike to eternal life.'

By the middle of the 6th century, Gaul—from the English Channel to the Pyrenees—was converted to Catholicism, but the remainder of Europe was not. However, not long after, the disciples of St. Benedict and St. Patrick were joining forces to renovate the face of Europe.

This period, in particular, witnessed the explosion of monasticism. The father of early monasticism was **St. Anthony**. Egyptian by birth, at age 20 he sold all of his possessions and gave the money to the poor. He then lived for twenty years in a deserted fort on the east bank of the

Nile. After he was discovered, others sought to imitate his example. In caves, among the rocks surrounding his hermitage, Christian monasticism was born.

However, there was no organized community life until St. Pachomius. In the course of his life in the 4th century, he founded eight monasteries and began to organize life in these settings according to detailed rules. Progress and meals were in common, while agricultural and industrial efforts at the monasteries also emerged. **St. Pachomius** is additionally credited with creating the first religious order. By the end of his life, there were already thousands of monks in monasteries that spread from Egypt to Syria, Asian Minor, and Europe.

The Middle Ages is generally considered to be the time between 590 and 1517. During this period, historians note that it became clearly recognized that the East was the East and the West was the West. The Church also realized that Greek was Greek and Latin was Latin.

The early Middle Ages (590-1048) saw the Church stretch out across the world, producing many great saints. **Saint Gregory the Great** (540-604) was the prefect of Rome when the Lombard invasion threatened the city. He had set out to evangelize England, but was called back to Rome when a great plague struck, killing Pope Pelaguis. Gregory the Great restored ecclesiastical discipline, administered papal properties wisely, and mediated a peace with the Lombard King. He is recognized as being responsible for the conversion of England through his dispatch of St. Augustine of Canterbury and for the restoration of Rome, which had been devastated by invasions, pillages, and earthquakes during the previous century. He wrote treatises, notably his *Dialogues*—a collection of visions, prophecies, and miracles of saints—as well as hundreds of letters. The Gregorian chant also bears his name. He is the last of the traditional Latin Doctors of the Church. Gregory the Great died on March 12, 604. St. Bede preserved the inscription in his tomb:

> In this tomb are laid the limbs of a great pontiff, who yet lives forever in all places in countless deeds of mercy. Hunger and cold he overcame with food and raiment, and shielded souls from the enemy by his holy teaching. And whatsoever he taught in word, that he fulfilled in deed that he might be a pattern, even as he spoke words of mystic meaning. By his guiding love he brought the Angels to Christ, gaining armies for the faith from a new people. This was thy toil, thy task, thy care, thy aim as shepherd, to offer to thy Lord abundant increase of the flock. So Consul of God, rejoice in thy triumph, for now thou hast the reward of thy works for evermore.

St. Bede provides us with this letter in which St. Gregory gives a lesson in Missionary methods:

In the year 601 **Gregory the Great** wrote the following letter to Abbot Mellitus, one of the second hand of missionaries sent by him to England:

> When Almighty God has led you to the most revered Bishop Augustine, tell him what I have long been considering in my own mind concerning the matter of the English people; to wit that the temples of the idols in that nation ought not to be destroyed; but let the idols that are in them be

destroyed; let water be consecrated and sprinkled in the said temples, let altars be erected, and relics placed there. For if those temples are well built, it is requisite that they be converted from the worship of devils to the service of the true God; that the nation seeing that their temples are not destroyed, may remove error from their hearts and knowing and adoring the true God, may the more freely resort to the places to which they have been accustomed.

And because they are used to slaughter many oxen in sacrifice to devils, some solemnity must be given them in exchange for this, as that on the day of the dedication, or the nativities of the holy martyrs, whose relics are there deposited, they should build themselves huts of the boughs of trees about those churches which have been turned to that use from being temples, and celebrate the solemnity with religious feasting, and no more offer animals to the devil, but kill cattle and glory God in their feast, and return thanks to the Giver of all things for their abundance; to the end that whilst some outward gratifications are retained, they may the more easily consent to the inward joys. For there is no doubt that it is impossible to cut off everything at once from their rude natures; because he who endeavors to ascent to the highest place rises by degrees or steps, and not by leaps....

The 6th and 7th century also witnessed many other evangelical successes through great saints and their works of courage and perseverance. **St. Columba**, known as the "apostle of Scotland" headed from Ireland to Northern Britain to convert the pagans there. His biographer gives us some insight into this great saint:

He had the face of an angel, his disposition was excellent, his speech brilliant, his deeds holy, his counsel admirable. He could not pass through the space of a single hour without applying himself either to prayer or reading, or writing or also to some manual labor. By day and night he was so occupied, without any intermission, in unwavered exercise or fasts and vigils that the burden of any of these labors might seem to be beyond human endurance. And amid it all, he showed himself affable, smiling, saintly. He carried the joy of the Holy Spirit in his inmost heart.

Another great Irish Saint, **St. Columban**, left Ireland in the year 589 with twelve companions and traveled to Gaul. He built a monastery there and soon had followers spread all over Europe. St. Columban's followers were seen as bringing to Europe a new level of achievement in the work of the Church. Ten of them went on to be venerated as saints.

We should also remember other great saints of the early Middle Ages:

St. Gall

St. Gall, a disciple of St. Columban, began a monastery that became one of the chief sites of learning and education in Europe for centuries.

St. Adrian

St. Adrian, evangelized the English in the mid-7th century with such success that some English historians say that it is he who should be known as the apostle of England, not St.

Augustine of Canterbury. He had a sincere love of the poor and he gave a horse the king had given him to a beggar.

St. Boniface

Originally named Wynfreid, Pope Gregory II changed his name to Boniface in honor of a holy martyr. St. Boniface achieved great success in his missionary work in Germany and was made a bishop. There is a popular story that when St. Boniface cut down a tree the local peasants thought to be sacred, the Oak of Thor, all the people converted to Christianity because St. Boniface was not struck dead by the gods.

By the year 800 a kind of loyalty between the Pope and Frankish kings reached a high point with the coronation of Charles (the Great) in Rome. However, the problem between the Eastern and the Western Churches continued to mount. By the late 8th century, a dispute over whether the Holy Spirit proceeds from the Father and the Son or just the Father heightened the tension. Other problems arose over the separation between Church and state as kings and secular rulers claimed the right to select and install priests and bishops without consulting the Pope. Thus, one of the issues regarding Christian rulers of state was to what degree they should be involved in spiritual or Church affairs. The rise of Islam also began during this time, and the Eastern Church was especially confronted with this danger.

The 9th century continued to witness the spread of the Christian Faith in northern and central Europe. **Pope Nicholas I**, the strongest Pope of the century, taught that the emperor's duty was to protect the Roman Catholic Church, not direct it. But because of invasions from Vikings in the North and Hungarians and Moslems from the east and south, Europe was falling into feudalism. This resulted in the decline of the western empire and the subsequent decline of the Western Church.

There was also a brief schism between Rome and Constantinople between 858 and 879. While some of the issues were resolved, these problems, along with lingering doctrinal disputes, eventually produced the great schism of 1054 between the East and West.

Toward the end of the 9th century, Islam was increasing its suppression of the Church in the East, and along with a decline in fervor within the monasteries, a general corruption and decline in both the Church and society were at hand. Yet, again, God's hand can be seen at work, for great Saints arose to begin missions that would eventually reverse the tide in the Church and in the world.

SS. Cyril and **Methodius** were brothers born in Greece in 826 and 827. Both lived in a monastery in 861, when emperor Michael III sent them to convert the Khazaars in Russia. In 863, the Patriarch of Constantinople sent the two brothers to convert the Moravians. They invented an alphabet called Glagolothic, which initiated Slavonic literature. To this day, the liturgical language of the Russians, Ukrainians, and Bulgarians is the one designed by these two saints—the "Apostles of the Slaves."

Approximately, one hundred years later, the people of Russia were converted by a man named Vladimir, who was called the "Great and Apostolic Prince." Moriravieff, a Russian historian gives us this account:

After his return to Kiev, the 'Great Prince' caused his twelve sons to be baptized and proceeded to destroy the monuments of heathenism. He ordered Perun to be thrown into the Dniepr. The people at first followed their idol, as it was borne down the stream, but were soon quieted when they saw that the statue had no power to help itself. And now Vladimir, being surrounded and supported by believers in his own domestic circle, and encouraged by seeing that his boyars and suite were prepared and ready to embrace the faith, made a proclamation to the people. 'That whoever, on the morrow, should not repair to the river, whether rich or poor, he should hold him for his enemy.' At the call of their respected lord all the multitude of the citizens in troops, with their wives and children, flocked to the Dniepr; and without any manner of opposition received holy baptism as a nation from the Greek bishops and priests. Some stood in the water up to their necks, others up to their breasts, holding their young children in their arms; the priests read the prayers from the shore, naming at once whole companies by the same name— Vladimir erected the first church that of St. Basil, after whom he was named—on the very mount which had formerly been sacred to Perun, adjoining, his own palace. Thus was Russia enlightened.

During the middle of the 10th century, the Holy Shroud was also transferred from Edessa to Constantinople. This event is seen as providential, for two centuries later Edessa was pillaged by the Turks. This, experts believe, would certainly have resulted in the destruction of the shroud.

While the 9th and 10th centuries were times that saw great evils pummel the church, hope and order were slowly re-emerging. The Church was going through a reorganization and a purification, all of which were the seeds of a coming time of glorious renewal and growth.

CHAPTER NINE

A TIME FOR HEROIC ACTION

The Church and the world changed dramatically over the next several centuries. The conflict between Church and State continued, as the Church struggled to maintain its sovereignty against the encroachment of kings and temporal rulers.

During this time, more and more people began to live in town and cities, which placed new demands on the Church. And the conflict in the Church between the East and West continued, leading up to the schism of 1054.
.
The following list outlines the major themes of the 11th, 12th, and 13th centuries:

> **The Church-State Relationship in the West**—The Popes of this period were constantly realigning themselves with different rulers and nations. This was done to preserve the autonomy of the Papal States and to maintain a balance of power in Europe. Some emperors such as Frederick I of the Hohenstaufen family even seized Rome, causing Pope Alexander III to flee. In England, Archbishop Thomas Becket of Canterbury was also forced into confrontation with King Henry II. St. Thomas Becket, who

fled from the conflict, returned only to be murdered on the steps of the altar in his cathedral at Canterbury.

The Crusades—While the Church was constantly struggling with secular rulers, the Crusades were equally taxing, if not more so. These "Holy Wars" were viewed as "just" attempts to liberate the Holy Land from Moslem control and to defend the Christian faith. Although the Crusades were initially well-intentioned, they became marred by the resulting brutality, as well as the damage between the Eastern and Western Churches.

The Culture and Theology Movement—The 12th century witnessed the beginning of Scholastic Theology, which sought to employ "reason" in understanding the mysteries of Faith.

At the same time, life in the monasteries and Cathedral Schools began to bring about new changes in the practice of the Faith. The earlier focus on Christ the King was replaced by a Crucified Christ, reflecting the people's own uncertain struggles. Likewise, devotion to Mary and the saints flourished, and worship increasingly centered on the Eucharist. The "real presence" of Christ became a focus and the term "transubstantiation" began to be used.

Heresies and Reform—As in the past, new interpretations of the Bible surfaced, causing groups of followers to abandon the teachings of the Church. In France, a group called the

Albigensians formed. These "new Manicheans" believed in two gods—one good and one evil, one who controlled the flesh and one who controlled the spirit. They adhered to a strict list of rules, which posed great danger to the faithful.

Another group of heretics, known as the Waldensians, also emerged. They attacked the fundamental dogmas of the Christian Faith and carried their errors to every country in Europe. Their heresies led to the Inquisition, which like the Crusades, has been the subject of debate for many Centuries.

Councils and Popes—The period of the 13th century gave rise to some of the most successful Councils of Bishops in Christian history. In 1215, the Lateran Council was called and in 1245 and 1274 the First and Second Councils of Lyons were held in France. A tremendously successful Jubilee Year or Holy Year was called in 1300. This was the first of its kind and attracted over a million pilgrims to Rome. Likewise, a string of great Popes emerged. Pope Innocent III was the first to take the title "Vicar of Christ" and recognize the need for new Orders of the Age. Pope Boniface III led opposition to State influence in the Church and proclaimed the ultimate authority of the Pope over both the Church and Christian orders in his famous edict, *Unam Sanctam*.

The Mendicant Orders—A great period of new orders also occurred between the 10th and

14th centuries. These orders responded to the movement of people from the country to the cities. Fr. Lawrence G. Lovasick, S.V.D., in his book, *Church History: The Catholic Church through the Ages*, outlines these new orders and their founding dates:

TABLE OF DATES OF NEW RELIGIOUS ORDERS (1084-1256)	
1084 Order of Carthusians	founded by St. Bruno of Cologne (d. 1101)
1098 Order of Cistercians	founded by St. Bernard (d. 1153) building on a group originally formed by St. Robert of Molesme (d. 1110)
1108 Order of Canons Regular of St. Victor	founded by William of Champeaux (d. 1122)
1120 Order of Canons Regular of Pre'montre'	founded by St. Morbert of Xanten (d. 1134)
1156 Order of Carmelites	founded by Berthold of Carmes (d. 1195) on Mount Carmel

1233 Order of Servites	founded by Bonfilio Monaldi and his companions (the Seven Holy Founders)
1256 Hermits of St. Augustine	various congregations that lived according to the Rule of St. Augustine were gathered together in this religious community by Pope Alexander IV.

To this day, these Orders of the Middle Ages have continued their work in the Church, inspiring and helping millions of the faithful.

But just as well known as these Orders are the great men and women, the great saints of this age, who rose up to lead the Church's renewal. In fact, many believe that in spite of the problems of this era, this period of the 13th century was the height of Christendom. This is because in almost every area of life, we can see the influence of the Church and the advancement of learning cultures and Christian Faith. Thus, the light of these times outshines the darkness.

But once more, it was the saintly men and women of this age that produced such great changes. And there were many of them:

> **St. Leo IX (1002-54)**, elected Pope in 1048, traveled all over western Europe to bring reform, earning the title of the "Apostolic Pilgrim." He instituted the proposal, which

stands today, that the Pope can only be elected by Cardinals.

Pope Gregory VII, formerly Hildebrand, was a guiding spirit of the Church for 23 years and carried on a relentless war of Church reform. A German historian provides us with a detailed description of this Pope:

Gregory VII was the 'marvel of his century,' and in some respects the greatest of all the Popes. He was not only the instrument of Providence for the reform of the Church, but also the savior of European society. By establishing the supremacy of the spiritual authority over the secular power–the Sacerdotium over the Regnum –he held in check the passions of the great ones of earth, the violent and lawless feudal aristocracy, who, if given free rein, would have thrust Europe back into Barbarism. His death did not compromise his work. His ideals and ideas lived after him and triumphed under his successors. The glories of Christianity in the twelfth and thirteenth centuries are the direct results of the policy of Hildebrand. 'The victory of the unarmed monk,' says the Protestant historian Gregorovius, 'challenges the admiration of the world with more right than all the conquests of Alexander, Caesar, or Napoleon. The Popes of the Middle Ages did not

wage their wars with lead and iron,
but with moral force alone. Compared
with a Gregory VII a Napoleon is
nothing but a sanguinary barbarian.'
(Geschichte der Stadt Rom in
Mittelalter, IV, p. 198)

St. Bruno, the founder of the Carthusians,
was born in Cologne around 1030. Ordained
in 1057, he began his order in 1084. Along
with six companions, his order embraced a
life of poverty, manual work, prayer, and
manuscript copying. In 1090, Pope Urban II,
his former pupil, brought him to Rome as
papal advisor. He was never formally
canonized because of the Cathusian aversion
to public honors, but Pope Leo X granted
permission for his feast in 1514 and his name
was placed on the Roman calendar in 1623.

St. Bernard of Clarvaiux, born in 1091, is
credited with founding the Cistercians in the
1112. He was extremely eloquent and
performed many miracles. Over 70
monasteries branched off the monastery at
Clairvaux, where the monks, besides being
known for their holiness, also achieved great
agricultural success. St. Bernard was
especially renowned as a peacemaker,
negotiating peace between rival bishops,
between bishops and their clergy, and between
the Emperor Lothar and his rebelling vassals.
He is known as "the last of the Fathers of the
Church."
St. Celsus and St. Malachy were influenced
by the teachings at Clairvaux. These two

monks brought reform to the Irish Church. St. Malachy became especially known for his reported prophecies of the Popes, from Celestine II (1143) to the last Pope.

St. Norbert of Xanten rivaled St. Bernard in fame and influence and was the founder of the celebrated Order of Regular Canons known as the Premonstratensians. He went on to found a monastery where some of the most illustrious men of the day begged the favor of living under St. Norbert's direction.

St. Dominic was born of noble parents in Calarvega, Spain, in the Year 1170. He was especially known for his preaching against the Albigensians and helped reform the Cistercians. He founded an order, known today as the Dominicans, that became known for theology and philosophy. He is also credited with being given the Rosary by the Virgin Mary during his battle with Albigensians outside of Toulocese in the early 13th century.

St. Francis was born in Assisi, Italy, in 1181, and has been called the "only true Christian since Christ." His parents were wealthy silk merchants, and Francis spent his youth in extravagant living. Later, he went off to war and was taken prisoner in 1202. After a serious illness, he experienced a vision of Christ that caused him to change his lifestyle. His ministry was especially devoted to a life of poverty and care for the sick and the poor. Soon, he attracted numerous disciples—some very wealthy. This lead to the founding of the Franciscan Order. In 1210, he received approval from Pope Innocent III for a Rule he had drawn up to direct his thousands of followers.

St. Francis was ordained a deacon, but never became a priest. He sought to convert the leader of the Moslems, but this effort failed in Egypt. Countless books record his life which are filled with stories of the supernatural. But most noted, according to Fr. Laux, is the account of St. Francis receiving the Stigmata:

Toward the end of his life, Francis voluntarily resigned the headship of his Order, which already numbered over five thousand Friars, so that he might have more time to devote to prayer and works of penance. His favorite place of retreat was Mount Alverna. On the feast of the Exaltation of the Cross, September 14, 1224, as he was contemplating the passion and death of Christ, he saw a seraph flying towards him. There was the figure of a man attached to a crow between the wings. After the vision disappeared, the hands and feet of the Saint were found to be marked with nails, and there was a wound in his side. He had received the sacred stigmata, the impress of the nails and the lance as a testimony to his oneness of spirit with Christ. Two years later, on the 4th of October, 1226, he died at Assisi amid scenes of touching simplicity, poor and bare like his Divine Master. He was canonized in 1228 by Pope Gregory IX.

St. Clare of Assisi was born in 1194. She was so impressed by a sermon of St. Francis of Assisi in 1212 that she ran away from home and received the habit from St. Francis. She is responsible for the founding of the Poor Clares and she was consulted by popes, cardinals and bishops. She died in Assisi on August 11, 1253, and was canonized two years later.

St. Elizabeth of Hungary was the daughter of Andrew II of Hungary. She was married at age 14 and had four children. She became well known for her charity and built a hospital at the foot of her family's castle. In 1228, after her husband died, she became a Franciscan tertiary. Her devotion to the sick, the aged, and the poor became well known, as did her life of exceptional poverty and humility. Upon her death in 1231, many miracles were reported at her tomb. She was canonized in 1235.

St. Albert the Great was born in Swabia, Germany, and studied at Padua. He became a Dominican and earned great acclaim for his intellect and learning. He later went to Rome where he served the Pope as his personal theologian. St. Albert was one of the great intellects of the age. Besides being a theologian, he was also a "nature" scientist. His knowledge of chemistry, biology, physics, astronomy, geography (one of his treatises proved that the earth was round) was considered encyclopedic. He also wrote considerably on logic, metaphysics, mathematics, the Bible, and theology. He is credited with pioneering the Scholastic method. Thomas Aquinas was his student. Pope Pius XI canonized him in 1931.

St. Thomas Aquinas was born in 1225 near Aquino, Italy. In 1244, he joined the Dominicans and was ordained in 1250. A master of theology, Thomas Aquinas taught at Naples, Orvieto, Rome, and Viterbo. Aquinas is probably considered the greatest theological master of Christianity and his thought continues to dominate Catholic teaching. His writings were incredibly voluminous and his *Summa Theologica* is considered the greatest exposition of theological thought ever written. Besides his extraordinary intellect, St. Thomas was also a mystic, experiencing visions, ecstasies, and revelations. Pope St. Pius V declared him a Doctor of the Church in 1567.

St. Anthony of Padua was born in Lisbon, Portugal, in 1195. He was ordained in 1220 and became a Franciscan in 1221. Known for his preaching, he preached all over Italy and became known for his success with heretics. He was declared a Doctor of the church in 1946 by Pope Pius XII, and is regarded by the faithful as the "Wonder Worker" for the many miracles brought through his intercession. He is also widely invoked for lost articles. Likewise, his depictions in art with the infant Jesus in his arms comes, reportedly, from an episode in which this event was actually observed.

St. Bonaventure was born in Bagnorea, Italy, in 1221. According to legend, he received his name from St. Francis of Assisi who cured him of a childhood illness. In 1238, he became a Franciscan. He received his doctorate of theology in 1257 and became an outstanding philosopher and theologian. He is known as one of the great minds of the medieval era. Known as the "Seraphic Doctor," he wrote numerous treatises, biblical commentaries, and sermons, as well as the official Franciscan biography of St. Francis of Assisi. He was canonized in 1482 and declared a Doctor of the Church in 1588.

CHAPTER TEN

GREAT SAINTS LEAD THE COUNTER REFORMATION

The Late Middle Ages (1300-1500) was again a time of decline for the Church. Bubonic plague, or "Black Death," swept through Europe during this period, killing approximately one-third of the population. But in Christendom, the Church witnessed an era of schism, great demands on the papacy, and marked mysticism.

The period began with what was known as Avignon Papacy, named after Avignon, France, where seven popes reigned between 1305 and 1377. Because of dangerous rivalries among Rome's noble families, French Pope Clement V began this "reign in exile" to seek protection from the French monarchy. The move also preserved peace between France and England.

This period was followed by the great Western Schism (1378-1417). During this period there was a succession of popes and anti-popes. The conflict was finally resolved with the Council of Constance (1414-1418).

Meanwhile, the seeds of the Protestant Reformation had been planted and were beginning to grow. John Wycliffe, a priest and professor at Oxford University, and a Bohemian priest named John Hus began to challenge the hierarchy of the

97

Church.   This also included a denial of the Church's Sacraments. In the year 1410, the errors of Wycliffe and Hus were condemned and Hus was excommunicated.

In the later half of the 14th century, a secular movement known as the" Renaissance" began in Italy and spread throughout Europe. This produced great changes in literature, culture, commerce, art, politics, and religion.   Several important discoveries also contributed to the sweeping changes brought about in the late Middle Ages. These were primarily the invention of gun powder in 1346 and the invention of the printing press, which significantly affected culture, politics, and religion. Thus, by the late 15th and early 16th centuries, a movement known as "humanism" was taking hold in the West.

This movement proposed that human beings should live life as fully possible on earth.   Indeed, nothing was to be mortified or expiated because of faith. From the beauties of nature to the great reservoir of "knowledge" in the physical, biological, psychological, and social sciences, the experience and "knowledge" of life were of primary importance.

The Church encouraged Christian humanism during this time, stressing that knowledge should be utilized in search of God. Of course, a great conflict soon developed, which extends to this day. The conflict involved the inevitable integration of humanistic thought into religion, society, and culture. Soon, the civilized nations of Europe began to embrace theories that God had nothing to do with the lives of human beings and that happiness was obtained by living without ethics, morals, and scruples.   A happy life was now measured by pleasure and success.

This, together with Luther's Protestant Reformation—which

includes the "radical reformation" of Calvin, other post-Luther heretics, and the reformation in England—signaled that the Catholic Church of the 16th century was at a crossroads. It needed reform and renewal. It needed spiritual awakening, and it needed the heroic men and women of the Age for the task.

Foremost among the saints that God providentially provided to rescue the Church and the times were St. Bridget of Sweden, St. Gertrude the Great, St. Bernadine of Siena, St. Catherine of Siena, and St. Vincent Ferrer.

St. Bridget of Sweden

St. Bridget was born in 1303 in Upland, Sweden. Early in her life, she experienced visions and was married at the age of fourteen. She bore eight children, one of whom was St. Catherine of Sweden. She founded a monastery in 1344, which marked the beginning of the Brigettine Order. Her visions lead her to involvement with the Kings, Queens, and Popes of her day, as she became known for her prophecies and her denunciations of those in high office. She died on 1372 and was canonized in 1391.

St. Gertrude the Great

Born in 1256, St. Gertrude was placed under the care of Benedictine nuns when she was five years old. When she was twenty-six, she began to receive many visions of Christ and wrote a book, *Revelations of St. Gertrude.* Along with St. Mechtilde, she also wrote a series of prayers that were very highly circulated. Her writings especially helped spread devotion to the Sacred Heart. Although never formally canonized, Pope Clement XII proclaimed that her feast be observed throughout the Church in 1677.

St. Bernadine of Siena

St. Bernadine of Siena was an orphan who was raised by his aunt. In 1400, he joined the Franciscans and was ordained in 1404. Known for his jury sermons, he preached all over Italy and attracted great crowds, especially for his denunciation of the rampant evil of the times. He also preached devotion to the Holy Name. He was canonized in 1450.

St. Catherine of Siena

St. Catherine of Siena, the youngest of twenty five children, began to experience mystical visions by the age of six. Refusing to marry, she devoted her life to prayer and fasting and became a Dominican tertiary when she was sixteen. Blessed Raymond of Capua was appointed her confessor. While on a visit to Pisa in 1375, she received the Stigmata. Over the years, she served as an advisor to the popes, and was involved in the great issues of the day such as the Great Schism. She recorded her mystical experiences in a book titled *The Dialogue,* and to this day is known as one of the greatest mystics of all time. She was made patroness of Italy in 1939 and declared a Doctor of the Church by Pope Paul VI in 1970.

St. Vincent Ferrer

St. Vincent, born in Valencia, Spain, joined

the Dominicans in 1367. He became a
professor and was involved in the struggles
that surrounded the Avignon popes. After
recovering from a serious illness in 1398,
during which he experienced a vision of
Christ, he became a great preacher. For the
next two decades, he traveled Europe
preaching penance and preparation for the
Last Judgment. He developed thousand of
followers. In Spain alone, he is attributed
with converting thousands of Jews and Moors.
He was canonized in 1455.

Talk of reforming the Church developed prior to the
Protestant reformation. Unfortunately, it was too little too
late. With the Church's eventual reform, however, came
many great saints. And the Church, through vast missionary
efforts from Africa to America, greatly expanded its
influence. This reformation was ignited by the founding of
new religious orders and communities, along with the renewal
of existing orders. In summary, a new quest for a holy,
religious clergy emerged. This lead to the founding of the
Jesuits by **St. Ignatius** of Loyola in 1534.

A Spanish soldier whose leg was shattered in a battle in 1521,
St. Ignatius read the life of Christ and a book of saints while in
recovery. This gave him tremendous spiritual joy. Inspired, he
chose six men to help him in his spiritual work—one of whom
was St. Francis Xavier, the great missionary of the Orient.

The Jesuits began by educating the poor and the illiterate in
the Faith. This eventually lead them to do the same with
princes and kings. The Jesuits also became great missionaries
as well. Beginning in 1541, **St. Frances Xavier** took the
Gospel of Jesus Christ to India and Japan. Afterwards, the

battle to intellectually defend the Catholic faith became a primary work of the Jesuits.

St. Peter Canisius of Germany wrote a catechism of the Catholic Faith that drew acclaim even from Protestants, while **St. Robert Bellarmine**, another great Jesuit theologian, became a leader of the reform at the Council of Trent.

Other orders emerged during this period of the Reformation and counter-reformation. A reformed branch of Franciscans known as the Capuchins was very influential, as were orders of religious women, such as the Ursuline Sisters and The Daughters of Charity.

After the Council of Trent concluded in 1563, the new spirit of the Church could be seen in such great saints as **St. Charles Borromeo**, who instituted radical reforms in his diocese to improve the morals and manners of both clergy and laity. He also provided religious instruction for children, built new seminaries, and established local synods and councils. This new spirit was evidenced as well in St. Frances de Sales, St. Jeannes de Chantal (1572-1641), and St. Vincent de Paul, who also contributed to leading the Church into a new era.

During this same period, great mystics such as **St. Teresa of Avila** and **St. John of the Cross** were being reinvigorated spiritually through their mystical experiences and devotion to prayer. St. Teresa founded seventeen religious houses and wrote several books. *Dark Night of the Soul*, a spiritual classic by St. John of the Cross, is still widely read.

As in the early days of the Church, when it struggled with the Roman empire, this period witnessed many heroic saints—of lesser fame, perhaps, but of equal importance for the times.

These were the Catholics who were martyred in defense of their beliefs.

This is illustrated in the sacrifice of the "Martyrs of Gorkum." In the year 1572, the Calvinists imprisoned seventeen priests and two lay brothers in Gorkum. They were then mutilated and finally hung for refusing to deny their belief in the Real Presence of Christ in the Eucharist and in Papal Supremacy. In 1865, they were canonized.

The efforts and sacrifices of the great saints of this period should serve as an example for all of us today. For, surely, their trials and their response can help us better understand what may lay ahead for the Church in its present crisis.

St. Ignatius

CHAPTER ELEVEN

THE NEW EVANGELIZATION

After the counter reformation, the next three centuries were very busy ones, not just with the continuation of the renewal but with exploration and evangelization of many new areas of the world.

The work in the New World centered in Central and South America and was carried out mostly by the Franciscans and the Dominicans. In Africa, the Dominicans, Jesuits, and Augustinians were present. While in Asia, **St. Francis Xavier** led the Jesuits in their efforts to evangelize Japan, India, and China. Again, all of this came at a great price. Especially in Japan, where in recent apparitions, the Virgin Mary tells us that an almost complete conversion to Christianity is coming.

In 1531, the mass conversion of almost ten million peasant Indians following the apparitions of Our Lady of Guadulupe certainly illustrates the missionary fervor of this period. This extraordinary event, brought about through the labors of the Franciscans, created a permanent foundation for the Church in the New World.

By the early 18th century, the evolution of Humanism was continuing to create havoc in the Church in Europe. Aided by secret sects known as the Society of Freemasons, the attacks on the Church involved influencing people through their livelihoods.

At the same time, temporal rulers continued their never-ending efforts to gain control of the Church. In France, a heresy known as Jansenism, which claimed God does not wish to save all souls, became widespread. Likewise, rationalism also emerged, which led to the denial of the very existence of God.

Thus, by the 18th century, the Church was at another crossroad—a profound crisis was approaching. Across Europe, a lack of belief was sweeping through the people. Decades later, this giant wave of atheism would produce the French Revolution. Meanwhile, the Freemasons, spurred on by such renowned rationalists as Rousseau and Voltaire—devotees of Jansenist, Blaise Pascal—stirred up the common people against the Church. Eventually, this led to the overthrow of the monarchy and an intense persecution of the Church. The result—the French Revolution!

Essentially, this revolution was driven by the impoverished French peasantry. Together with the French bourgeoisie, who were also inspired by the writings of Rousseau and Voltaire, the French peasantry directed their assault at Catholicism. They came to believe, through the activities of the Masonic lodges, that Catholicism was the true cause of the social injustices of the times.

As a result of the French Revolution, the Catholic Church in France was paralyzed. New laws were enacted to damage religious life, while the Catholic calender was abolished. And as before, the martyr's blood of this age flowed in the streets, especially during the September Massacres of 1792 and the Reign of Terror in 1793. By 1804, Napoleon Bonaparte emerged as the ruler of France. In order to maximize his power, he quickly approved negotiations with the Pope—

negotiations that resulted in the 1802 Concordat between France and the Holy See.

Again, as in the past, great saints rose up in service of the Church. They rose up in fidelity to defend the Faith. And as always, God made certain that good sprang forth from evil.

Indeed, one of the positive results of Jansenism was devotion to the Sacred Heart of Jesus. Around the year 1650, **St. John Eudes** first began to promulgate this devotion. Born in Normandy, France, in 1681, St. John Eudes joined the Congregation of the Oratory of France in 1623. He resigned from the Oratorians in 1643 and founded the Congregation of Jesus and Mary (the Eudists) at Caen. After this, he set up a series of missions and established new seminaries at Lisieux in 1653 and Roven in 1659. In 1668, he composed the *Mass for the Sacred Heart.* He also wrote two books, *The Devotion to the Adorable Heart of Jesus* (1670) and *The Admirable Heart of the Most Holy Mother of God*, which he completed a month before his death on August 19, 1680.

Around the same time, a humble French Visitation nun, named **St. Margaret Mary Alacoque**, revealed a series of revelations that were given to her concerning the Sacred Heart of Jesus. St. Margaret Mary was born in Burgandy, France, in 1670. She was bedridden with rheumatic fever for five years until she was fifteen. At the age of twenty, she began experiencing visions of Christ. During these visions, Christ informed her that she was His chosen instrument to spread devotion to His Sacred Heart, and devotions known as the "Nine Fridays" and the "Holy Hour" emerged. Subsequently, she entered a convent at the age of twenty-four and professed her vows the next year.

The devotion for the Feast of the Sacred Heart was also given to her, but for a great while, her superiors refused to follow the instructions for these revelations. She, St. John Eudes, and her spiritual director Blessed Claude La Colombiere are now referred to as the "Saints of the Sacred Heart" for their efforts to promote this devotion. St. Margaret Mary was canonized in 1920.

Another great saint of the time was **Saint Alphonsus Liguori** (1796-1787). He received his doctorate in both canon and civil law at age sixteen. After practicing law for eight years, he decided to become a priest and joined the Orations. He was ordained in 1726. In 1732, he moved to Scala and founded the Congregation of the Most Holy Redeemer (the Redemptorists). Known for his devotion to missionary work, St. Alphonsus devoted his time to preaching missions in rural areas and small villages. In 1762, he was appointed Bishop of Saint Agata dei Goti, where he set about to reform the clergy, the monasteries, and the entire diocese.

Because of a series of controversies, St. Alphonsus experienced a deep spiritual depression during the last few years of his life. But this period was replaced by a time of peace and joy in which he experienced visions and ecstasies and performed miracles. St. Alphonsus wrote many books, including the *Glories of Mary* and his notable *Moral Theology*. He was declared a doctor of the Church in 1871 by Pope Pius IX.

St. Paul of the Cross (1694-1775) had from his youth a strong devotion to the Passion of Jesus Christ. To inspire his colleagues with the same devotion, he founded the Congregation of the Passion in 1747. Their badge of Passion—black habits—quickly became known throughout the world.

A contemporary of St. Paul of the Cross was **St. Leonard of Port Maurici**, (1676-1757). He was a Franciscan who for forty-four years preached in every province of Italy, converting numerous souls with fiery and eloquent sermons.

St. John Baptist de la Salle (1651-1719), a director of the Sisters of the Holy Infant Order—an order devoted to the instruction of poor girls—founded the "Christian Brother Schools." This organization prepared teachers for village schools. He was also a pioneer in training schools and reformatories.

The conflict that most divided the Church during this period was the issue of individual judgment vs. ecclesial authority. Likewise, suppression and infidelity were true signs of the times. And these signs were pointing to a future storm of unparalled opposition.

St. Frances de Sales

CHAPTER TWELVE

THE CHALLENGE OF SECULARISM

A new world was born after the French Revolution—a world based on political participation, freedom of expression, and representative government. While most of the nations of Europe took strong measures to uphold their monarchies, in light of what occurred in France, the period of alliance between Church and State was coming to an end. Great changes were taking place. This meant that the role of the Catholic Church was to be radically redefined.

The most grievous question facing the Church at the beginning of the 19th century, and one that it still faces today, was how to respond to the "liberal" changes in society. Emerging from the dust of the French Revolution, liberalism, especially in politics, was creating a new order.

In politics, liberalism favored representative government, religious toleration, separation of Church and State, freedom of the press, and secular education. Likewise, liberalism also favored individual freedom of conscience and the right to openly express ideas and beliefs–whether they were true or not. In a free market, truth and error were equally offered to the consumer.

By the early 19th century, the Church had already condemned liberalism. Pope Gregory XVI wrote in his encyclical, *Mirari Vos* (1832), that Liberalism was allied with the "skeptical philosophy of the Enlightenment" and was harmful to the Church. But by 1850, the forces of liberalism had grown so strong that the history of the Catholic Church as a political force in Europe was at an end. However, with the losses of the Papal States and the rise of liberal constitutional governments, the Church was now better suited to focus on its spiritual mission.

The rapid onset of changes in the 19th century produced successive waves of disruption within the Church. In England and Germany, groups of Catholics advocated that the Church reform itself in light of so many scientific advances and philosophical changes. However, Catholic Church leaders, skeptical of reforms that they felt were tainted by rationalism and the Enlightenment, countered that this type of reform could only damage the Faith.

Pope Pius IX published a *Syllabus of Errors* in 1864 which outlined the dangerous ideas the new freedom of thought presented to Catholics. However, opponents of the Church quickly labeled it as opposed to modern thought and culture. Despite the opposition, Pope Pius IX continued his efforts to remind Catholics that they should look to the Church for guidance and truth. He understood that society at large, by the mid-19th century, was becoming an open forum of opinions. And he felt this was causing the faithful to believe that the Church no longer possessed God's revelation of Truth.

Responding to this crisis, Pius IX attempted to clarify certain points of the Faith. In 1854, he proclaimed, as a doctrine of the Faith, that Mary, the Mother of Christ, was conceived immaculately without Original Sin. He also called the First Vatican Council together in 1869 to discuss the relationship between faith and reason and the primacy and the teaching infallibility of the Pope.

From this, two constitutions were passed: (1) *Dei Filius*, which asserted the ultimate authority of God's revelation and that nature and reason are subordinate to grace and faith, and (2) *Pastor Aeternus*, which declared the infallibility and primacy of the Pope. The latter declaration was seen as essential in light of the history of the Church, noting how God, through great shepherds, had guided His Church through confusing and difficult times in the past. The Council had hoped to also illuminate the role of the bishops, clergy, and laity, but the onset of the Franco-Prussian War in 1870 brought it to an abrupt end.

While the 18th century certainly witnessed the unfolding of the worldwide apostasy that now has a stranglehold on the entire human race, God's work in the world was also spreading. Early in the century, Pope Pius VII reestablished the Jesuits. Likewise, many other new religious orders arose such as the Christian Brothers, the Sisters of Charity, the Marianists, the Marists, the Sisters of Loretto, the Paulists, the Salesians, the Society of the Divine Word, and the White Fathers. These new orders, and the re-energized existing orders, led a determined effort to revitalize Catholic social ministries, educators, and missionary work. This, in turn, was certainly an invitation by God to bring forth the saints that the times so desperately needed.

And indeed many were ready for the challenge!

St. John Vianney was one who responded to the need for reawakening the faith. Known as the Cure of Ars, John

Baptist Vianney was born on May 8, 1786. After many difficulties, he was ordained in 1815, and in early 1818 he was appointed Cure of Ars, where he spent the rest of his life.

At Ars, he tirelessly labored to help his parishioners. His focused on their indifference to religious teachings, waging war especially on immorality. Over time, he became a legend as he eventually converted the entire village through his expertise as a confessor and a spiritual director. On three occasions he attempted to leave Ars in order to pursue solitude, but each time he returned to aid his people who sought him in ever increasing numbers. He was canonized in 1925 and is the Patron of Parish Priests.

St. Clement Holbaurer was a Redemptorist priest who revived the Church in southern Germany. Born in 1751, and ordained in 1785, St. Clement spent twenty years working with the Poles, the Germans, the Protestants, and Jews. He worked among the poor, built orphanages and schools, and sent Redemptorist missionaries to Germany and Switzerland. In 1808, he was imprisoned and then exiled to Austria. He founded a Catholic college there and became instrumental in revitalizing the Catholic faith in Germany. He also played an important role in defeating an effort to establish a national German church. He is the Patron Saint of Vienna.

Perhaps one of God's most chosen souls of the nineteenth century was **St. Catherine Laboure**. Born in 1806, she joined the Sisters of the Charity of St. Vincent de Paul in 1830. Almost immediately, she began to receive a series of apparitions of the Virgin Mary at the Ru du Bac convent in Paris. In the apparitions, the Virgin Mary told St. Catherine that evils of every kind would come into the world and that the Church would be persecuted. Not long after the first apparition, riots broke out throughout France bringing to fulfillment the prophetic words given to her.

St. Catherine also was instructed by Mary to have a medal struck. This medal, because of the number of miracles associated with it, became known as the Miraculous Medal. St. Catherine died in 1876 and her body to this day is incorrupt.

In England, a convert named **John Henry Newman** initiated a campaign called the Oxford Movement. Newman led a wave of friends and disciples into the Church through his writings which sought to return the Church of England to Rome. Ordained a priest in Rome, Newman returned to England where he founded the English Congregation of the Oratory of St. Phillip Neri at London and Birmingham. After more than 30 years of writings and speaking on a vast array of religious subjects, his acclaim was recognized by Pope Leo XIII, who made him a cardinal in 1879. Newman is considered one of the great masters of English prose and his *Apologia pro Vita Sua* is also considered an unsurpassed religious autobiography. Likewise, his *Dream of Gerontius* ranks next to Dante in expressing the Catholic penetration of eternity.

The following is one of Cardinal Newman's sermons titled *The Second Spring*, which he preached at St. Mary's College, Oscott, at the First Provincial Synod of Westminster, July 13, 1852:

> Three centuries ago, the Catholic Church, that great creation of God's power, stood in this land in pride of place. It had the honors of nearly a thousand years upon it; it was enthroned in some twenty sees up and down

the broad country; it was based in the will of a faithful people; it energized through ten thousand instruments of power and influence; and it was ennobled by a host of Saints and Martyrs ....

But it was the high decree of heaven, that the majesty of that presence should be blotted out....No longer, the Catholic Church in the country; nay, no longer I may say, a Catholic community—but a few adherents of what had been. 'The Roman Catholics'—not a sect, not even an interest, as men conceived of it—not a body, however small, representative of the Great Communion abroad—but a mere handful of individuals, who might be counted like the pebbles and detritus of the great deluge, and who, forsooth, merely happened to retain a creed which, in its day indeed, was the profession of a Church. Here a set of poor Irishmen, coming and going at harvest time, or a colony of them lodged in a miserable quarter of the vast metropolis. There, perhaps, an elderly person, seen walking in the streets, grave and solitary, and strange, though noble in bearing, and said to be of good family, and a 'Roman Catholic.' An old-fashioned house of gloomy appearance, closed in with high walls, with an iron gate, and yews, and the report attaching to it the 'Roman Catholics' lived there; but who they were or what they did, or what was meant by calling them Roman Catholics, no one could tell— though it had an unpleasant sound, and told of form and superstition. And then, perhaps, as we went to and fro, looking with a boy's curious eyes through the great city, we might come today upon some Moravian chapel, or Quakers' meeting-house, and tomorrow on a chapel of the 'Roman Catholics'; but nothing was to be gathered from it, except that there were lights burning there, and some boys in white, swinging censers; and what it all meant could only be learned from books, from Protestant Histories and Sermons; and they did not report well of the 'Roman Catholics' but, on the contrary, deposed that they had once had power and had abused it. And then, again, we might, on one occasion, hear it pointedly put out by some literary man, as a result of his careful investigation, and as a recondite point of information, which few knew, that there was this difference between the Roman Catholics of England and the Roman Catholics of Ireland, that the latter had bishops, and the former were governed by four officials, called Vicars-Apostolic....

Such were the Catholics of England, found in corners, and alleys, and cellars, and the housetops, or in the recesses of the country; cut off from the populous world around them, and dimly seen, as if through a mist or in twilight, as ghosts flitting to and from, by the high Protestants, the lords of the earth.

St. John Newman, the third of six children, was born in 1811 in Bohemia. He was ordained in New York in 1835 and began his service for the Church as a missionary in upstate New York. He later joined the Redemptorists and his work took him to Pittsburgh, Baltimore, and finally Philadelphia. He was consecrated the fourth Bishop of Philadelphia in 1852. He reorganized his diocese, and was a special advocate of Catholic education. The two catechisms he wrote were endorsed by the American bishops at the first Plenary Council in 1852. In 1977, he was canonized by Pope Paul VI, becoming the first American male saint.

St. Elizabeth Ann Seton was another American saint of this era. Born in New York City in 1774, she helped to found the Society for the Relief of Poor Widows with Small Children in 1797. In 1803, she was widowed with five children after her husband died in Pisa, Italy. Returning to the United States, she became a Catholic. In 1809, along with four companions, she founded the religious community of the Sisters of St. Joseph and a school for poor children near Emmitsburg, Maryland. This led to the far reaching Catholic parochial school system in the United States. She took her vows on July 19, 1813. She also founded the Sisters of Charity, which at the time of her death in 1821 numbered some twenty communities throughout the United States. She was canonized by Pope Paul VI in 1975, becoming the first American born saint.

Francis Xavier Cabrini was born in 1850 in San Angelo Lodigiano, Italy. She was orphaned at age eighteen and decided to pursue the religious life. After success in founding the Missionary Sisters of the Sacred Heart, which was devoted to the education of girls, she responded to an invitation by the Archbishop of New York to work with Italian immigrants in America. For the next 27 years, in spite of great obstacles, she traveled extensively and her congregation spread all over the United States, Italy, South America, and England. By the time of her death in 1917, there were more than fifty hospitals, schools, orphanages, and other foundations in existence. She was the first American citizen to be canonized.

St. Thérèsè of Lisieux was born at Alencon, France in 1873. The youngest of nine children born to Louis and Zelie Martin, St. Therese moved to Lisieux with her father and sisters after the death of her mother. She was refused admission to Carmel, but was admitted one year later. Taking the name "Therese of the Child Jesus," she devoted herself to prayer and meditation. After becoming afflicted by tuberculosis, she bore her illness with great courage and recorded under obedience, the story of her childhood and her life in the convent. *The Story of a Soul* became one of the most widely read modern autobiographies and attracted a tremendous following to "her little way." Known as "the Little Flower," she was canonized in 1925 by Pope Pius XI. Over 2,000 churches throughout the world bear her name, and in 1992 her parents were beautified by Pope John Paul II.

Perhaps one the most influential and significant figures the 19th century was **Pope Leo XIII.** The successor of Pope Pius IX, Pope Leo sought to restore the leadership of the papacy and the influence of the Catholic Church throughout the world. A great diplomat, Pope Leo set about to establish conciliation with modern society and learning. By making John Henry Newman a cardinal and by striving hard to act as a friend of democracy—instead of condemning its errors— Pope Leo XIII moved the Catholic Church forward in the eyes of the world at a critical time in history. The great Pope also opened the Vatican archives to researchers, which again was seen as a positive step for the Church.

Most of all Pope Leo XIII defined the times through his great encyclicals, especially *Rerum Novarum*, which defended justice and better working conditions for workers. Poe Leo

XIII also wrote twelve apostolic letters on the Rosary, preparing in a mystical way for Mary's apparitions at Fatima, where she announced she had come as "Queen of the Most Holy Rosary."

Through his wisdom, Pope Leo XIII succeeded in bringing the Catholic Church into the modern world. It was a policy of conciliation, while carefully reaffirming the value of traditional Catholic theology and guiding it against modern errors. This was critical for such decisive times. Certainly, the world of the 20th century would hold challenges unlike any before. And in the end, only the wisdom of the Catholic Church would prove to be the answer.

CHAPTER THIRTEEN

FROM FATIMA TO DIVINE MERCY

Although **Pope Leo XIII's** record of accomplishment was extraordinary, he is probably best known by the average Catholic for his 1884 vision.

After saying Mass on October 13th, the Pope reportedly fell into a frozen, suspended state that left his attendants fearful that he had been stricken with a health problem. However, upon his recovery, the Pope reported overhearing a conversation between Satan and God. It was a conversation that revealed an agreement between God and the devil which permitted Satan to "try" God's people for one century.

Confirmed at Medjugorje by visionary Mirjana Soldo as being true, that century is known now to be ours—the 20th century. In retrospect, we certainly can see that if there ever was a century of a major confrontation between good and evil, ours certainly fits the bill. From World War I to the Russian Revolution of 1917, from the horrors of the Great Depression to the holocaust and global annihilation of WWII, the 20th century reads like a script from a long war movie. Death on the battlefield, death on the streets, death in our homes, and death in the womb—the major events of this century seem to have lead from one form of genocide to another.

Likewise, along with the great advances in science and technology, the 20th century has been marked by rapid changes leading to moral disintegration. **Pope St. Pius X** saw the handwriting on the wall early in the century as he sought to strengthen Catholic worship and to protect the Church from modern errors. He moved for more religious education of the youth and changed the age for receiving Holy Communion to the age of reason. He unified the Code of Canon Law and ordered the Catholic Church in France to give up all its property assets to the government rather than to submit to its control. This in turn provided a great spiritual renewal. More than anything else, Pius X's resolve to crush modernism in the Church must be noted. In his 1901 encyclical *Lamentabili Sane*, the propositions of the modernists were condemned. This was followed by his encyclical *Pascendi Dominici Gregis*, which led in 1910 to all Catholic clergy and pastors having to swear an oath to reject modernist teachings.

Not long after, one of the most significant events of the 20th century occurred in Fatima, Portugal—the Virgin Mary appeared to three shepherd children. And these apparitions, fully approved by the Church in 1930, can only be described as extraordinary in their miraculous nature and prophetic call. Mary's words at Fatima foretold great misery for the world if it did not convert. But Our Lady also promised that a glorious era of peace was ahead and that this promise was unconditional.

The next twenty years saw the end of World War I and the start of World War II. Meanwhile, tens, if not hundreds of millions of people died from the tyrannies of Fascism, Communism, and Nazism. The Catholic Church also suffered through a civil war in Spain in 1936 and atheistic governments tried to eradicate Catholicism in Russia, China, and Mexico. Once more, Pope Leo XIII's prophetic vision of a century of war between the forces of heaven and hell continued to be fulfilled.

The second half of the 20th century has not witnessed a world war, but its legacy of death is even more frightening. Hundreds of smaller wars have occurred or are still taking place, while a different kind of war emerged—the war on the unborn. According to the Blessed Virgin Mary, in her words to the visionaries (as well as verifiable data), more than fifty million abortions are occurring each year throughout the world. This holocaust is unparalled in human history and cries out—the prophets of today insist—for vengeance before the throne of God.

An almost endless list of additional sorrows has also entered the world in the last fifty years. But the most tragic is the break-up of the family. This has created a society of chaos, with blood flowing in the streets and in the homes of almost every free nation. In the East, where communism still maintains tight control over hundreds of millions, atheism has stripped the people of their hope and faith in God. Along with the West, the entire planet now attempts to function without any real sense of the presence of God. Thus, the errors which originated in the Middle Ages have finally brought the world to the brink of disaster.

The popes of the 20th century have certainly fought heroically through this decline. From Pope Benedict XI to Pius XII, the papacy has remained at the forefront in vigorously condemning abuses of every kind. Picking up where his predecessors had left off, Pope **Pius XI** condemned atheism and communism in his encyclical letter, *Divine Redemptores*, issued on the feast day of St. Joseph the worker in 1937.

Likewise, **Pope Pius XII** struggled courageously to combat both Communism and Nazism. At the same time, he warned Catholics of the dangers of the new "historical" theology in his encyclical *Humani Genesis*. Pius XII is especially remembered for his encyclical *Mystici Corporus Christi*, which revolutionized the Catholic view of the Church. This letter encouraged Catholics not to look at the Church as a human institution but as the "mystical body of Christ on earth."

The successor of Pope Pius XII also changed the face of the world with his bold and direct action. **Pope John XXIII** was a man of vision, especially in his understanding of the need for the Church to come of age in the modern world. John XXIII envisioned a "new Pentecost" and responded to this by calling for a worldwide conference of Catholic bishops. He encouraged the Council to "find meaningful, positive, and fresh ways, for stating the Church's age-old doctrine." Which is exactly what happened. The Council formulated documents that were both favorable to Catholic tradition and applicable to the needs of our times.

Pope Paul VI brought Vatican II to a successful conclusion and many movements of renewal sprung up in the Church. However, the increasingly secular and godless culture of the world maintained its share of challenges in the Church. Likewise, the problem of Communism continued to directly confront the Church and its mission.

After the sudden death of **Pope John Paul I**, **Pope John Paul II** began his papacy as the first non-Italian pope elected in centuries. His first encyclical, *Redemptor Hominus*, called the world to focus on Jesus Christ as the ultimate solution to its problems.

The Pope then began an unparalled effort of traveling to more nations than any Pope ever before, while carefully guiding a strategy designed to resist and defeat Communism in the East and the "Culture of Death" in the west. Affirming his dedication and consecration to the Virgin Mary, Pope John Paul II, like Pope John XXIII consistently proclaims that a "new advent" is on the horizon. With faith and hope, the Pope foretells the complete and total renewal of the world which will soon come, he says, through the Holy Spirit.

Again, as in the past, the 20th century has witnessed the rise of many great souls. Although, the future will probably reveal an unprecedented number of saints from this period, such names as Maximillian Kolbe, Faustina Kowalska, Pier Frassati, Joan Molla, Theresa Neumann, Padre Pio, Martha Robin, Matt Talbot, Jacinta Marta, Francisco Marta, Marcel Callo, Joseph Moscate, and Mother Teresa already stand out.

But it is the life and martyrdom of **St. Maximillian Kolbe** that perhaps paints the best picture of our century and its call for heroic leadership. Born in Poland in 1894, Kolbe joined the Conventual Franciscans, taking the name Maximillian. He took his vows in 1911 and founded in 1917 the Militia of Mary Immaculate in Rome to advance devotion to Mary. In 1925, about 25 miles from Warsaw, he founded Niepokalanow ("Cities of the Immaculate Conception") to house more than eight hundred religious. Similar efforts were made in India and Japan.

Then, in 1941, Maximillian Kolbe was arrested by the Nazis who had invaded Poland. He was imprisoned in their infamous death camp of Auschwitz. There, he voluntarily took the place of a married man with a family who was one of ten victims randomly selected to be executed in response to a prisoner's escape. Fr. Kolbe died on August 14, 1941, by a lethal injection of Carbolic Acid. In 1982, he was canonized by Pope John Paul II.

St. Maria Goretti

CHAPTER FOURTEEN

SECULAR SAINTS

It is no secret that most talk of saints immediately conjures up images of religious men and women. These are the priest and nuns who, responding to God's call to holy orders, proceed to great heights of sanctity and are immortalized by the Church.

But the Church teaches that God raises up saints in all walks of life. Indeed, whether you are a housewife or a farmer, you can achieve great sanctity while living in the world. The Church records a long list of such secular saints who have overcome extraordinary difficulties to achieve holiness.

Among such saints are mothers, fathers, doctors, lawyers, blue-collar workers, single people, soldiers, teachers, servants and even prostitutes.

Joan Carol Cruz's monumental work, *Secular Saints* (TAN Books, 1989), includes 250 such canonized souls. Listed below are the accounts of ten secular saints:

St. Michelin of Pesaro

Married at the age of 12, Michelin was widowed by the time she was twenty. But being fond of pleasure, she continued a carefree and worldly life. Then Michelin opened the doors one day for a holy woman named Syriaca. This produced a great conversion in her life. She denounced worldly pleasures and became a Franciscan tertiary. This change was drastic and led her to giving away all her possessions and to begging in the streets for food. As a result of this, she was considered mentally imbalanced and her embarrassed relatives had her committed to an asylum. She endured all of this with great patience and love and was finally released. She returned to helping the poor and the lepers, and toward the end of her life she was given mystical experiences involving Our Lord and His passion. She was canonized in 1737.

St. Isadore

St. Isadore was born in Spain the towards the end of the 11th century. Born in extreme poverty, his parents sent him at an early age to a wealthy land owner near Madrid. Isadore married and worked as a farmer, suffering trials and hardships in what remained a poor situation. Over time, it became Isadore's practice to attend Mass each morning before going to the fields. Because he was often late for work, his owner decided one day to investigate these reports for himself.

To his amazement, he observed that while Isadore was late for work, his work was always done. Then while he was watching, he witnessed a series of extraordinary sights. Unseen hands would guide Isadore's hands as he led the white oxen across the field. On another occasion, angels were witnessed plowing on either side of Isadore. During this, Isadore would be observed praying. Upon seeing this, his employer came to view Isadore as a chosen soul. Other miracles were witnessed over the years.

Isadore was also known for his generosity to the poor. He died on May 15, 1130. Forty years later, when his body was transferred, it was found incorrupt. Down through the centuries, great miracles on behalf of Spain's royalty were attributed to Isadore's intercessions. And because of these miracles, Spain's royalty petitioned for Isadore's canonization. In March of 1622, Isadore was canonized with such well known saints as St. Ignatius, St. Francis Xavier, St. Teresa of Avila and St. Phillip Neri. He is venerated as the patron of peasants, farmers, and day labors.

Blessed Margaret of Castello

Born blind and deformed, Blessed Margaret came from a noble and wealthy family. Upon her birth, the family was reportedly overwhelmed with grief. She was viewed as a shameful disgrace and every effort was made to keep her deformities a secret. Her parents wanted nothing to do with her, so a servant was trusted with raising her.

Because she was drawn to prayer at a very young age, her parents had her sent to a church at the age of six where she was to permanently reside as a recluse. Special building arrangements were made to confine her to the building. She suffered great cold in the winter and extreme and suffocating heat in the summer. For thirteen years she was imprisoned at the church.

During this time the priest discovered the blind girl's mind was illuminated by great graces which gave her a deep knowledge of the Faith. She would also practice secret mortifications.

After hearing of miraculous cures at the tomb of a Franciscan tertiary named Fra Gracome, Margaret's parents took her to Rome in hopes of finding a cure. But after several hours, Margaret was still not cured. Her parents abandoned their blind daughter in the church and returned home.

For years she was cared for in Rome by different families. She then joined a religious convent where her life was so exemplary that she was asked to leave because it made the other sisters feel guilty.

Public ridicule and contempt continued to plague her, but she was again asked to join another religion community. Here she is said to have memorized the 150 Psalms of David, the Office of the Blessed Virgin, and the Office of the Holy Ages. She passed from meditations to contemplation and practiced strict mortifications.

Margaret also embarked on missions of

helping the poor and the sick. She is credited with such great devotion to St. Joseph that she is recognized as one of the pioneers in devotion to him.

Many miraculous stories about Margaret have survived—from floating ecstasies to healings. Even after her death, while an argument erupted over her burial, the left arm of her body is said to have reached out of the coffin and touched an ill little girl. The little girl was instantly healed of deafness and she could walk for the first time. Canonized in 1609, Margaret's body remains incorrupt.

St. Elzear and Bl. Delphina

At birth, Elzear's mother offered him to God. She begged God to never allow her son to commit a serious sin. The development of this virtue was continued under his uncle, William of Sahran, who was the abbot of St. Victor's at Marseille—a monastery Elzear attended.

Delphina was an orphan. Like Elzear, she was educated by her aunt who was an abbess. The two were married at Chateau-Pont-Michel and decided on their wedding day to live as brother and sister. The two lived a life of heroic witness to the message of Scriptures. They endured insults and attacks by keeping their eyes on Christ and by prayer. Most of all, they were especially known for their holy household. Elzear wrote up the following regulations for his home:

Everyone in my family shall daily hear Mass, whatever business he may have. If God be well served, nothing will be wanting....Let no persons be idle. In morning a little time shall be allowed for meditation, but away with those who are perpetually in the church to avoid doing their work. This they do, not because they love contemplation, but because they want to have their work done for them....When a difference or quarrel arises, let the scriptural precept be observed that it be composed before the sun goes down. I know the impossibility of living among men and not having something to suffer. Scarcely a man is in tune with himself one whole day; but not to be willing to bear with or pardon others is diabolical, and to live with enemies and to render good for evil is the touchstone of the sons of God....I strictly command that no officer or servant under my jurisdiction or authority injure any man in goods, honor or reputation, or oppress any poor person, or damage anyone under color of doing my business. I do not want my castle to be a cloister or my people hermits. Let them be merry, and enjoy recreation at the right times, but not with a bad conscience or with danger of transgressing against God.

Elzear who admitted to never having committed a mortal sin, died on September 26, 1323. Fifty-three years later, he was canonized by his own godson, Pope Urban V. Delphina lived for another thirty-five years after her husband's death. Both St. Elzear and Bl. Delphina were members of the Third Order of St. Francis, and, therefore, are particularly venerated by the Franciscans.

St. Julian the Hospitable

The story of St. Julian is one of the most compelling of all time. Julian was of noble birth and left home at a young age to find adventure. Taking up service for a noble prince, he was rewarded for his gallantly by receiving a rich widow and her castle.

One day, upon returning home to his castle, he discovered two people in his bed. Thinking the worst, he drew his sword and slew them both. But he soon discovered that it was actually his own mother and father he had killed. They had come in search of him and were resting in his bed at his wife's request.

Thrown into despair, Julian vowed never to rest until he had knowledge that God had pardoned him for his sins. He and his wife then journeyed to a great river where they established a hospital. The pious couple made many charitable efforts on behalf of the poor, the sick, and the homeless. Finally, after taking care of a leper one day, the man suddenly said to Julian, "Julian, Our Lord hath sent me to thee and sendeth thee word that He hath accepted thy penance." Many hospitals in the Netherlands are dedicated to St. Julian. He is considered the patron of innkeepers, travelers, and boatmen.

St. Maria Goretti

The third child of Assunta and Luigi Goretti, Maria Goretti was born on October 16, 1890. Because of financial hardship, the Goretti family was forced to move from Corinaldo to Colle Gianturco, near Rome. Here they became acquainted with the Cimareeli family and the Serenelli family (which consisted of the father, Giovanni, and his son Alessandro). All three families then moved to Ferriere di Conca, a place near Nettuno.

The Serenelli and Goretti families shared a townhouse there and worked the land. One year after arriving, Luigi Goretti contracted malaria and died. Because her mother was now forced to work in the fields, nine year old Maria assumed the duties of the household. Besides being obedient and hard working, young Maria was also very spiritual. She prayed often and practiced mortification, suffering in silence and sometimes hunger.

On the morning of July 5, 1902, twenty year old Alessandro Serenelli, who had been harassing Maria, began to make improper advances to her. After being rejected by her, Alessandro produced a knife and threatened

Maria. However, Maria still would not submit, stating it would be a "sin against the law of God and he would go to hell." Alessandro then stabbed her 14 times. On her deathbed, Maria spent her last hours praying for Alessandro and stated "for the love of Jesus, forgive him...I want him to be in Paradise with me.

Alessandro received a prison sentence of thirty years. Afterwards, he testified at Maria's cause of Beautification. Maria Goretti was canonized on June 24, 1947. And in 1979, Pope John Paul II visited her shrine and exhorted today's young people to look to Maria Goretti as an example of purity in such a permissive society. Indeed, Maria Goretti is a great model for the youth of the world.

St. Godelieve

The youngest of three children, St. Godelieve was born in Belgium in 1049.

While preferring the religious life, Godelieve was forced to marry Bertolf of Gistal. Following their wedding ceremony, Godelieve journeyed only to find her husband's mother waiting for them with great anger. The mother insisted that the marriage be halted, and she confined Godelieve to a narrow cell.

Goldelieve eventually escaped and revealed what had happened to her. But the authorities, in trying to help, only made matters worse. They forced Bertolf to reconcile with is wife. But afterward, he ordered the servants to drown her. Since he would be away at the time, he believed no one could prove that he killed Goldelieve.

Bertolf soon remarried, but the daughter of this marriage, Edith, was born blind. Miraculously, healing occurred when her eyes were bathed in the water Goldelieve was drowned in. This caused Bertolf to experience a true conversion. He then traveled to Rome to obtain absolution, and finally entered into monastic life.

Edith, at Bertolf's request, erected a Benedictine Abbey near the pool where Godlelieve had died. Because of so many miracles, Godelieve's body was exhumed fourteen years after her death in 1084. Throughout Belguim, Godelieve's relics are venerated to this day and her intercession is especially sought in cases of eye or throat disorders and for maintaining or re-establishing peace in families.

St. Isabella of France

Princess Isabella was born in March 1225. Her father was Louis VII King of France, her mother, Blanche of Castile. From childhood, Isabella was very pious. She was also blessed with exceptional intelligence which permitted her to study natural history, religion, medicine, logic, and languages. Although very beautiful, she declined marriage in order to remain a virgin for "the sake of Christ." Isabella became very prayerful, often riding before dawn to pray and continuing her devotions until midday. She then would serve the poor and sick people. Although she never entered an order, she established a convent near Paris. The remainder of her life was dedicated to using her money and property to help charities of the poor. During her last few days, she experienced ecstatic visions and spent whole nights in contemplation. The feast of St. Isabella is celebrated on August 31st.

Blessed Louis Morbioli

Louis Morbioli was born to a bourgeois family in Bologna, Italy, in 1433. He was a very handsome young man who married at a young age. But although married, he reportedly was given to avarice, ambition, and sensuality. In fact, one biography notes that he was notorious for "loose living." In fact, he was regarded as scandal by all who knew him. But in 1462, he became seriously ill and experienced a death bed conversion.

Immediately, he changed his fashion and cut his hair. After making provisions for his wife, he set about to do penance for his past sins. He began to minister to the poor and the sick, and he taught Christian doctrines to the young and uneducated.

After his death many miracles were attributed to his intercession. His cultus was acknowledged by Pope Gregory XVI in 1842.

And because the Carmelites claim that Louis became a tertiary of their order after his conversion, he is still venerated by this order and the people of Bologna.

Blessed Antonia Mesina

Antonia Mesina was born on June 21, 1919 in Orgosolo, Italy. She was the second of ten children. Her childhood was marked by great piety and obedience. She received her first holy communion at age seven. Because of her mother's illness, she had to leave school after only four years. She then assumed many responsibilities for the family. On May 17, 1935, when Antonio was 16 years old, she and a friend, Annedda Castangia, set out to gather wood for the oven.

While the two girls were walking through the woods, a student from the school where Annedda attended crossed their path. A few minutes later, he returned from the rear and grabbed Antonia. He forced her to the ground, but Antonia broke away twice. The third time, the would-be rapist grabbed a rock and repeatedly struck Antonia's head and face. Annedda screamed and went for help, but when she returned, Antonia had already been brutally beaten to death. According to the autopsy, she had not been violated.

Like St. Maria Goretti, she had died a martyr of holy purity. Her attacker was captured and sentenced to death. Antonia Missina was beatified on Sunday October 4, 1987, by Pope

John Paul II. Also beautified on that day were two more 20th century lay saints and martyrs: Blessed Marcel Callo and Blessed Piesina Morosini.

St. Francis of Assisi

CHAPTER FIFTEEN

THE GREAT SAINTS

The information on saints is not recorded with the highest degree of accuracy. According to experts, it is based on myth, legend, tradition, distorted or comprehensive biographies, hearsay, and other sources of information. However, in most cases, the Church has carefully weighed substantial amounts of material in reconstructing a candidate's life.

The sheer number of saints on record is in the thousands. From Apostles to popes, warriors to mothers, this list reflects an impressive cross section of almost every kind of person that ever walked the face of the earth. However, some saints were extremely instrumental at particular times in history for the defense or advancement of the Church. We can call these the "Great Saints." Listed below are the condensed biographies of twenty of the greatest saints in Church history:

St. Denis

The early Christians in Gaul (France) suffered greatly at the hands of the Romans. Almost all of them were killed in a great persecution by the emperor Valerian. After this terror was over, the Pope decided he must send some missionaries to preach the Gospel and to encourage the surviving Christians.

He chose a man named Denis, who was learned in the Christian Faith. Denis and two friends—Rusticus, a priest, and Eleutherius, a deacon—traveled the roads of Gaul to the area now known as Paris. They settled here and, despite the dangers, built a church. They made so many converts that they angered, not only the Romans, but the local pagans. Finally, they were taken to a hill overlooking the city. There they were beheaded for refusing to sacrifice to the pagan gods.

Years later, a great church was built on that location so that everyone in France would remember Denis, the first Bishop of Paris, the Patron Saint and "Apostle of France."

St. Helen

When the Roman emperor Constantius died in the year 306, the Roman army declared his son Constantine the new emperor. Constantine's mother was named Helen. Helen had lived in Britain and was a pagan before converting to Christianity.

After Constantine won a great victory under "the sign of the cross," he declared Christianity an official state religion and became baptized. His mother was also one of the first to be baptized. When she learned about Christ's crucifixion she began to wonder what had happened to the actual Cross of Jesus Christ.

Finally, though she was eighty years old, she decided to go to Jerusalem to find the True Cross. Since it had been 300 years since Christ had died, Calvary had been built over by the Romans and was now covered with statues of Roman gods. But because her son was the emperor, she was able to have this building torn down and removed from the hill. The excavation then began to locate Christ's True Cross.

Finally, after receiving a dream, she searched near a rock cistern and unearthed three crosses. Since they all looked the same, no one could tell which one was Christ's Cross. But again, inspired through prayer, Helen decided to lay a sick man on each cross. When a sick man was laid on the third cross, he was instantly healed. Helen, convinced that this was the True Cross, ordered a great church built on the site. She then took the wood of the cross and two nails back with her. In Rome, she had another church built where the relics were then placed.

St. Brigid

St. Brigid of Ireland was born in the 5th century. Her father was a chieftan and her mother a slave. From earliest childhood she was seen as blessed, as miracles seemed to occur around her. Bridget desired at an early age to become a nun. Finally, along with some friends, she offered herself in the service of God and the bishop. The bishop reportedly said to the young women, "You shall be called the Sisters of Mercy." He then gave them white robes and instructed them on their mission. In Ireland, her convent soon became the center of religion and learning. She also founded a school of art and a book production center of unparalled quality. St. Brigid was said to have been guided by the angels, and her fame spread far and wide. She is the Patroness of Ireland.

St. Benedict

St. Benedict was born in the year 480 in the hilly country of central Italy. At the age of fourteen, he went to Rome to study. Scandalized by the lifestyle of the Romans during this period, Benedict fled the city to live in a cave. For three years he lived in a cave near other hermits among the Subraco Mountains.

Benedict eventually left the cave and became the abbot of local monastery. He then established a strict code of conduct for monastic life. This code, known as the Benedictine Rule, eventually became adopted by thousands of monks in monasteries throughout the world. Although St. Benedict founded many monasteries, the most famous is at Mount Cassino. Here at the foot of the mountains, Benedict's sister Scholastica, founded a convent where women could live under the same Benedictine Rule. Today, his rule and teachings are still used by many and his medal is widely circulated.

St. Athanasius

Perhaps one the greatest saints in Church history was St. Athanasius. Born in Egypt in 295, St. Athanasius was a child when Alexander, the future bishop of Alexandria, took notice of him. Alexander took him into his household and began to train him for the priesthood. At the age of 25, Athanasius wrote his famous treatise, *on the Incarnation of the Word of God.* By the age of 30, he exercised great authority at the Council of Nicea. But most of all, St. Athanasius is most known for being the "scourge" of Arianism, the first heresy in the Church which denied the Trinity. The Arians knew from the beginning that Athanasius would be difficult to deal with. They tried threats, promises, and calumny. All sorts of ridiculous charges where raised against him. A woman who accused him of immorality could not even recognize him. Yet, in spite of everything, he persevered and saved the Church. His heroic determination is so significant that the entire story must be reviewed. John T. Delaney in his *Dictionary of Saints* wrote the following of St. Athanasius:

> Probably born of Christian parents at Alexandria, Athanasius was well educated, especially in Scripture and theology. He was ordained a deacon, and became secretary to the Bishop of

Alexandria in 318. Athanasius was present with his bishop at the Council of Nicaea, which condemned Arianism and excommunicated Arius. After Alexander's death in 327, Athanasius was elected bishop of Alexandria. In addition to his rule as bishop of the city, he became the spiritual head of the desert hermits and of Ethiopia. He was immediately confronted with a revival of Arianism in Egypt, its rapid growth throughout the Mediterranean world, and the continued schism of the Meletians, who supported the Arians. In 330, Eusebius of Nicomedia, a supporter of Arius, persuaded Emperor Constantine to direct Athanasius to admit Arius to communion. When Athanasius flatly refused, Eusebius incited the Meletians to use every means to discredit Athanasius. They charged him with various crimes, and when he was cleared at a trial before Constantine, they accused him of murdering Arsenius, a Meletian bishop everyone knew was alive and in hiding. Aware of this, Athanasius refused the summons of the Meletians to attend a synod to answer the preposterous charge, but was obliged, by the Emperor's command, to attend a council at Tyre in 335. The council was completely dominated by his enemies and presided over by the

Arian who had usurped the bishop of Antioch. Athanasius was found guilty, and though the Emperor, after an interview with Athanasius, repudiated the findings of the Council, he later reversed himself. Athanasius was banished in 336 to Trier in Germany. Constantine died in 337 and his Empire was divided among his sons—Constantine II, Constans, and Constantiud. Constantine II then recalled Athanasius, but Eusebius denounced Constantine II to Constantius (Alexandria was in Constantius' portion of the Empire) for sedition. He succeeded in having Athanasius again deposed at a synod in Antioch and an Arian bishop introduced into his See. A letter from this synod asking Pope St. Julius to confirm its actions was followed by another one from the orthodox bishops of Egypt supporting Athanasius, a copy of which was also sent to the bishops in the West. When Gregory, a Cappadocian, was installed as archbishop supplanting Athanasius, riots broke out in Alexandria. Athanasius then went to Rome to attend a synod. Pope Julian I agreed to hear his case. However, when none of the Eusebians showed up for the synod, it proceeded with its deliberations and completely vindicated Athanasius—a decision that was confirmed by the Council of Sardinia. It was while he was in Rome, that Athanasius established close contact with the bishops of the West who supported him in his struggles. He was unable to return until Gregory died in 345, and Constantius, at the urging of brother Constans, the Western Emperor, unwillingly restored Athanasius to his See. But when Constans was assassinated in 350, Constantius, now Emperor of both East and West, moved to exterminate orthodoxy and deal with Athanasius once and for all. Constantius called councils at Arles in 353 and at Milan in 355 to condemn Athanasius and to exile Pope Liberius to Thrace, where he was forced to agree to the censures. Arianism was now in control, but Athanasius continued to resist until one night soldiers broke into his church, killing and wounding many in the congregation. He fled to the desert and was protected there by the monks for the next six years while an Arian bishop, George of Cappadocia, occupied his See. It was during these years that he wrote many of his great theological works. When Constantius died in 361, George was murdered soon after, to be briefly succeeded by Pistus. When the new Emperor, Julian the Apostate, revoked all of his predecessor's banishments of bishops, Athanasius returned to Alexandria. Soon, however, he came into conflict with the new Emperor when he opposed his plans to paganize the Empire and he was again forced to flee to the desert. When Julian was killed in 363, Athanasius was brought back by Emperor Jovian. But following his death, after an eight-month reign, Athanasius was forced into hiding for the fifth time when the new Emperor, Valens, banished all orthodox bishops in 365. He revoked the order four months later, and Athanasius, after seventeen years of on-and-off exile, returned to his See and spent the last seven years of his life in Alexandria building a new Nicene party. This party secured the triumph of orthodoxy over Arianism at the General Council of Constantinople in 381. St. Athanasius died in Alexandria on May 2. He is one of the great figures of Christianity. A Doctor of the Church and the " champion of orthodoxy," he resolutely opposed one of the greatest threats Christianity ever faced –Arianism–and persevered in the face of trials and difficulties, that at times, seemed insurmountable. A friend of the monks Pacholius, Serapion, and St. Antony, whose biography he wrote, he aided the ascetic movement in Egypt and was the first to introduce knowledge of monasticism to the West. Through it all, he guided his flock and found time to write treatises on Catholic doctrine that illuminated the areas in which he wrote. Among his outstanding works are *Contra gentes* and *De incarnatione verbi Dei,* defenses of the Incarnation and Redemption written early in his life (318-23), and the major treatises he produced in exile: *Apologia to Constantius, Defense of Flight, Letter to the Monks*, and a *History of the Arians*. He did not write ·the Athanasian Creed, but it was drawn from his writings, probably by some unknown cleric. He is a Doctor of the Church.

St. Francis de Sales

St. Francis de Sales was born 1567 in Savory. He studied at the Jesuit College of Clemont in Paris from 1580-1588. At age 24 he received his doctorate of law. While offered a senatorship, he declined to pursue the religious life and was ordained in 1593.

Despite stiff opposition and threats on his life, he converted thousands back to Catholicism. He became Bishop of Geneva in 1602 and was one of the outstanding leaders of the Counter Reformation. He was a great preacher and went on to found many schools. Known for his wisdom and intellect, he founded the Order for the Visitation and wrote several spiritual classics, including *Introduction the Devout Life*, and *Treatise on the Love of God*. He was declared a Doctor of the Church in 1877 and is the Patron Saint of the Catholic Press.

St. Teresa of Avila

St. Teresa was born in Avila, Spain, in 1515. She was taught by the Augustian nuns but was forced to leave the convent because of ill health. In 1536, she became a Carmelite and was professed in 1538.

St. Teresa is especially known for her visions, which she at first doubted. In 1562, she founded the St. Joseph convent in Avila for nuns who desired an enclosed spiritual life rather than the relaxed style of the age.

In 1567, her supervisor gave her permission to begin more convents. She eventually founded sixteen. At her second convent, she met St. John of the Cross, who then took over the task of forming Carmelite reformed monasteries. Over the years, St. Teresa wrote many letters and books that are widely regarded as classics. Some of them are her *Autobiography* (1565), *The Way of Perfection* (1573), and *The Interior Castle* (1577). St. Teresa is generally recognized as one of the great mystics of all time. She was known to be intelligent, hardheaded, charming and demanding. She was declared a Doctor of the Church in 1970.

St. Audrey

St. Audrey, whose name was Etheldra, was born a princess in the little Sulfolk village of Exning. She married young but her husband died and she soon married again, despite her desire to become a nun. She was then married to Prince Egfried of Worthumbra, but she remained unhappy. Both were virginal marriages.

Finally, her husband gave her permission to leave and to become a nun. But soon he changed his mind and pursued her. He finally caught her about to cross the sea at a place called Coldeburgh Head, where a great rock jutted out to sea. But as the King and his men approached, a great tide of water separated him from her. The King watched for the tide go down, but for days it stayed the same. Finally, he became convinced that God was protecting her.

St. Audrey eventually returned to Ely, where she built a church that eventually became a great Cathedral. Over the centuries, the people there have worn little ribbons in honor of St. Audrey's refusal of court splendor for the simple life of the village.

St. Bernard of Clarvaiux

St. Bernard was born at Fontaines les Dijon in Burgandy in 1090. After a frivolous youth, he decided to pursue the religious life. In 1112, he and thirty one friends and relatives traveled to a monastery in Citeaux that followed the

Rule of Benedict. Three years later he was asked by a friend to form a monastery at Langres, where he would be Abbot. Soon, he attracted scores of disciples. This led to some sixty-eight monasteries. His reputation grew, and he became one of the most influential men in Europe. Kings, Popes and, Princes sought his consultation. He was a leader in convincing the Lombards to accept Lothaire II as Emperor and led the opposition to the rising exalation of reason.

Besides being involved in many of the great events of his times, Bernard also was a great preacher and writer. His mystical writing, especially *De Diligendo Deo* is considered one for the great medieval mystical works of the times. He was canonized in 1174 and declared a doctor of the Church in 1830.

St. John of the Cross

Born on June 24, 1542, St. John was born Juan de Yepes y ALvarez, the youngest son of a silk weaver. When he was seventeen, he began studying at the Jesuit College in Medina. In 1563, he joined the Carmelites at Medina and was ordained in 1567.

He met St. Teresa of Avila on a visit home to Medina and accepted her invitation to join efforts in effecting the reform of her Order. Taking the name "John of the Cross," his involvement in the conflict between the Discalced and Calced Carmelites eventually led to his imprisonment at Toledo. After nine months in prison, he escaped and went on to found a college in Baeza. In 1582 he was elected Prior of Granada.

After another round of controversy, he was exiled as a simple monk to a monastery in Andalusia, where he contracted a fever and died.

St. John of the Cross is recognized as one of the great mystics of all time, and his writings are considered spiritual classics, especially his *Dark Night of the Soul*. He was canonized in 1726 and proclaimed a doctor of the Church by Pius XI in 1926.

CHAPTER SIXTEEN

ST. JOSEPH, THE GREATEST OF ALL THE SAINTS

Can we say there is one saint in the history of the Church, excluding the Blessed Virgin Mary, that truly can be labeled the greatest of all the saints? This question undoubtedly has been raised, not just among devoted followers of individual saints, but among great Church scholars and historians who have felt intellectually compelled to ponder this question. Indeed, names of the more meritorious candidates immediately come to mind: St. Peter, St. Paul, St. John the Baptist, St. John the Evangelist, St. Mary Magdalene, St. Gregory the Great, St. Leo the Great, St. Francis of Assisi, St. Anthony of Padua, St. Joan of Arc, St. Thomas Aquinas, St. Teresa of Avila, St. Louis de Montfort, St. Thérèsè of Liseux, and perhaps another dozen or so worthy nominees.

But if one saint truly emerges, clearly having the most support for the honor of being recognized as the greatest saint in the history of the Church, it is St. Joseph, the husband of Mary and the foster father of Jesus Christ.

According to the historical record that has emerged over the last two centuries, no saint has drawn more acclaim than St. Joseph. His unique role in the history of salvation is incontestable. But scholars have pieced together a personal portrait of the great Saint through various sources that illuminate St. Joseph's extraordinary and perhaps unparalleled uniqueness as a servant of God. From thoroughly acknowledging the many divine favors granted to St. Joseph by God, to confirming his outstanding virtues of humility, fidelity, obedience, purity, patience, and devotion, the modern portrait of St. Joseph portrays him as a human being who was the most Christ-like of all human beings. Ironically, this is despite the fact that Christ's public life did not begin until after St. Joseph's death.

Therefore, St. Joseph practiced a Christocentric lifestyle without ever having read the New Testament or having heard the Messiah publicly preach His message of love. While certainly the home of the Holy Family must have been a rich environment for the love and message Christ brought into the world, there is no evidence that Jesus schooled St. Joseph in His law of Love. Rather, according to scholars who have studied St. Joseph's life, as well as accounts by mystics who have received visions of his early life, St. Joseph clearly grew in divine grace and continuously earned more and more extraordinary favors from God. This enabled the hidden saint to quietly go about his daily work earning a livelihood for the two central persons of the Redemption entrusted to his care, all the while perfecting a role that the Church now rightfully proclaims as an exemplary model of Christian ideals.

Although our present age asserts that St. Joseph deserves honor and glory, this has not always been the case in the Church. The silence of the early Church on Saint Joseph has often been noted. No specific images of the saint were found in the catacombs and some of the most respected early indexes on the historical evolution of the early Church fail to mention his name.

Early understanding about St. Joseph was largely influenced by a very well studied and documented Christian work known as the Apocrypha. The Apocrypha was composed of six documents that achieved almost Gospel status in the early Church. However, later they were rejected from the canonized text of the New Testament by the Church and gradually their importance waned. They contained much of what early tradition handed down about St. Joseph, such as stories of the miracles that accompanied the espousal of Mary and Joseph, and the list of marvels that marked the Holy family's sojourn in Egypt.

The first of the Church Fathers to examine the life and role of St. Joseph was St. Augustine. His writings comprised what theologians describe as the foundation of all theological teaching on this matter. Drawing primarily upon Scripture, St. Augustine's teaching established the following summary of the life of St. Joseph:

(1) Joseph is not the natural father of Jesus.

2) Joseph receives the rights of fatherhood from God. This is evidenced by the command of the angel that Joseph bestow Christ's name.

(3) Joseph receives his position as father ultimately because he is the husband of Mary, who is the Mother of Jesus.

(4) Joseph is likewise the father of Jesus by reason of the spiritual affection with which he accepts Christ at his Son.

(5) Since Jesus was conceived within the marriage of Joseph, although not by the seed of Joseph,

the saint is far more than an ordinary adoptive father.

(6) Jesus received His human ancestry and His human hereditary rights through Joseph.

(7) The Child Jesus is given to Joseph as well as to Mary, but to Joseph through Mary.

(8) The fatherhood in the moral order which Joseph exercises over our Lord does not encroach on the fatherhood as possessed by the Eternal Father over the Second Person of the Trinity. On the other hand, the Divine origin of Christ does not take away from His special father-son relationship with Joseph.

(9) Augustine calls Joseph "virgin father" of Jesus, signifying that Joseph himself was a virgin and that he received Christ within his virginal marriage with the most selfless paternal love, free of all concupiscence.

St. Augustine's theological thought, according to scholars, was barely expanded upon for centuries. In the medieval period, St. Thomas Aquinas' *Summa Theologica* established a more explicit formulation of Augustine's views. He argued that St. Joseph was given to Mary to protect her honor, to veil the virginal birth from men and Satan, and to provide a home and sustenance for mother and child.

Toward the end of the Middle Ages, we find a growing attraction to St. Joseph. John Gerson, a known scholar of the time, presented a classic in literature on St. Joseph before the Council of Constance. And one of his pupils, St. Bernadine of Siena, provided much of the material on the saint for the breviary. After this, we find Masses and Offices in honor of St. Joseph.

But it is with St. Teresa of Avila that an apologetic argument for devotion to St. Joseph emerges in a formidable way. Her writings added depth, understanding, and refinement to the growing love for St. Joseph. Likewise, she clearly established his immense power of advocacy.

As St. Joseph became a source of power for public figures to call upon, the 17th century Church continued to produce clarification on St. Joseph's role. John Solbieski, a Polish patriot soldier and king, undertook his great crusade against the Turkish forces at the gates of Vienna in 1683 in the name of St. Joseph. Likewise, scholars note that St. Joseph's place in the Church emerged more publicly with the Protestant Reformation, for he was now called upon to defend the Church.

With the outbreak of rationalism in the 19th century, a series of papal pronouncements revealed the emerging cult of the Saint by giving him increased liturgical honors. Petitions from all over the world begin to reach Rome asking the Pope to declare St. Joseph the Patron of the Universal Church and to raise his feast to a higher rank in the liturgical calendar. Sixteen years to the day after the Dogma of the Immaculate Conception (December 8, 1870), the Bull *Quemadmodum Dues* proclaimed St. Joseph's universal patronage. This was one of the first acts of a Pope under the new definitions of

Papal Infallibility and Primacy. One year later, the letter *Inclytum Patriarcham* elaborated more extensively on the theology of the declaration. Pope Pius IX called to mind how Pope Sixtus IV wished the feast of St. Joseph to be inserted in the Roman Missal and Breviary, how Pope Gregory XV ordered that a feast day should be observed throughout the whole world, and how Pope Clement X and Clement XI added to this order.

After this, a series of papal pronouncements furthered the role of St. Joseph in the Church. Pope Leo XIII expanded on the subject, while Pope Benedict XV wrote a letter commemorating St. Joseph's Patronage. Pope Pius XI ended his encyclical on *Atheistic Communism* by an appeal to the working class of the world to adopt St. Joseph as their special protector against the errors of communism, while Pope Pius XII placed on the calendar a new feast of the great saint, that of *St. Joseph the Worker.* In 1961, Pope John XXIII published a special apostolic letter on St. Joseph. In it he recalled one by one the acts of his predecessors in favor of St. Joseph and named him Patron of the Vatican Council. He also directed that the name of St. Joseph be included in the Roman Canon of the Mass.

Since Vatican II, the cult of St. Joseph has continued to grow. Pope Paul VI on June 12, 1978, declared Alfred Besette— better known as Brother Andre, the "miracle man of Montreal"—to be venerable. This little man was perhaps more responsible than any other person of the 20th century for the continued growth of the cultus of St. Joseph. In Montreal, Brother Andre spent decades spearheading the construction of a magnificent basilica known as St. Joseph's Oratory. On May 23, 1982, pope John Paul II beatified Brother Andre.

During his pontificate, Pope John Paul II has continued to extol the virtues of St. Joseph. In his 1989 apostolic letter, *Redemptoris Custos*, Pope John Paul II commends everyone to St. Joseph:

> One hundred years ago, Pope Leo XIII had already exhorted the Catholic world to pray for the protection of Saint Joseph, Patron of the whole Church. The Encyclical Epistle *Quamquam Pluries* appealed to Joseph's fatherly love...for the Child Jesus and commended to him, as 'the provident guardian of the divine family,' 'the beloved inheritance which Jesus Christ purchased by His Blood.' Since that time—as I recalled at the beginning of this Exhortation—the Church has implored the protection of St. Joseph on the basis of 'the sacred bond of charity which united him to the Immaculate Virgin Mother of God,' and the Church has commended to Joseph all of her cares, including those dangers which threaten the human family.
>
> Even today we have many reasons to pray in a similar way: 'Most beloved father, dispel the evil of falsehood and sin...graciously assist us from heaven in our struggle with the powers of darkness...and just as once you saved the Child Jesus from mortal danger, so now defend God's Holy Church from the snares of her enemies and from all adversity.' Today we still have good reason to commend everyone to Saint Joseph.

While certainly the Church does not definitively state that St. Joseph was the greatest saint of all, it is evident that it has moved to bring recognition and devotion to St. Joseph in an unparalleled fashion. Except for the Virgin Mary, no saint has been so venerated and promoted. This in itself may be seen as sufficient testimony to establish who this great servant of God was in the eyes of the Church. In addition, according to the eminent Irish theologian Michael O'Carroll C.S.S.P., whose own 1963 book *Joseph, Son of David*, is considered an important contribution to contemporary literature on the great saint, theologians have come to agree that indeed, St. Joseph rightfully deserves to be called the "greatest saint of all times."

But perhaps the words of St. Teresa of Avila contain, in summary, the best explanation for why so many believe St. Joseph is the greatest saint of all:

> I took for my advocate and lord the glorious Saint Joseph and commended myself earnestly to him; and I found that this my father and lord delivered me both from this trouble and also from other and greater troubles concerning my honour and the loss of my soul, and he gave me greater blessings than I could ask of him. I do not remember even now that I have ever asked anything of him which he has failed to grant. I am astonished at the great favors which God has bestowed on me through this blessed saint, and at the perils from which he has freed me both in body and in soul. To other saints the Lord seems to have given grace to succour us in some of our necessities but of this glorious saint my experience is that he succours us in

them all, and that the Lord wishes to teach us that, as he Himself was subject to him on earth (for, being his guardian and being called his father, he could command him), just so in heaven he still does all that he asks. This has also been the experience of other persons whom I have advised to commend themselves to him; and even today there are many who have great devotion to him through having newly experienced this truth....

St. Joseph and the Christ Child

CHAPTER SEVENTEEN

THE SPECIAL GRACES GIVEN ST. JOSEPH

According to theologians, St. Joseph received magnificently divine graces and favors from God which contributed to his exalted stature in the Communion of Saints. Many of these supernatural graces are mysteries, as Scripture reveals little of the life of St. Joseph. But as St. Joseph was predestined by God for the dignity of Mary's husband and foster-father of Jesus, we are able to conclude that these divine favors were unparalleled in any other creature except for the Blessed Virgin Mary.

The "United Greeks," in their praises of St. Joseph, speak of him as "more than a saint," or rather, as "pre-eminently a saint." This is because of the superabundance of graces he received and because of his perfect correspondence with those graces. In fact, ecclesiastical authorities state that because it is so certain that St. Joseph exceeded all saints in graces, it is then far from rash to conclude that he has exceeded them in glory. This is especially conceded because Joseph was associated with the Incarnation, which was of a higher order than any other sacred mystery.

Over the centuries, as the study of St. Joseph's life progressed, experts have come to believe that St. Joseph's life was so sanctified that God must have bestowed upon him special graces while he was in the womb, and then again after his death.

According to many theologians, it was fitting that St. Joseph, because of his special role in the mystery of the Incarnation, be speedily cleansed from stain of Original Sin. All in him needed to be holy and pure. Therefore, the conflict in him between the flesh and the spirit needed to be extinguished. Like Jeremias and St. John the Baptist, many theologians reason that St. Joseph was freed before birth from the stain of Original Sin. Over the centuries, mystics have asserted this in their revelations. This was also necessary, they note, for him to be the fitting spouse of the chaste Mary and to fulfill Scripture's assertion that Jesus "was subject to them" (Mary and Joseph) (Lk 2:5).

Indeed, only by St. Joseph being free of Original Sin, theologians argue, could Jesus truly "be subject" to St. Joseph. This reasoning is then also applied to understanding why St. Joseph had to exceed all the other saints in greatness. Fr. P. Paola Segneri, an eminent theologian of the 19th century, writes concerning St. Joseph and this mystery:

> How can anyone suspect that Joseph, who by affinity and by offices was so closely united to the universal source of all sanctity, was made participant thereof in a lower degree and in less perfection that those who were much further removed from it? For this reason, then, we may well conclude, with very solid grounds of probability, that he was not only sanctified in his mother's womb, but also confirmed in grace and exempted from all malice, so that no man on earth—let us boldly

affirm it—was ever holier than St. Joseph. (It must be noted that this does not include the Blessed Virgin Mary who was not sanctified from original sin in the womb but was immaculately conceived. That is, she was conceived without Original Sin.)

To emphasize their argument that St. Joseph was truly the greatest saint ever, theologians often discuss his life in comparison with St. Peter and St. John the Baptist, who also was believed to have been pre-sanctified in the womb from the stain of Original Sin. These two great saints are considered to be the most worthy of comparison since they, too—because of the charges confided to them and their titles—were extraordinary saints.

According to the great theologian of the Middle Ages, Suarez, St. Joseph again is clearly found to be of the greatest rank. While Suarez notes that an Apostolic ministry occupies the first rank of various ministries in order of grace, it must be considered of a lessor order than that of the Hypostatic Union, which in its kind is more perfect and surpasses the Apostolic ministry. While St. Joseph holds third rank in the order of the Hypostasis Union, writes Suarez, he "is superior even to Peter, who is first in the Apostolic hierarchy."

Suarez further explains that "between the ministry of the Apostles and that of St. Joseph there exists this difference: the former is immediately for men, to conduct them to Christ; that of St. Joseph is immediately directed to Christ Himself; in order to preserve Him for men, and is therefore so much the more noble and sublime."

Pope Benedict XIV concluded the same. Writes the Holy Father, "These graces, these spiritual prerogatives, of Joseph are great, are eminent, are most certain, and are so exclusively his that they have not been given to any other saint." Other theologians have also pointed out how St. Peter and St. Paul, as great as they were, held only two titles: Servants and Apostles of Jesus Christ. These two titles, wrote St. John Chrysostom, "are more excellent than all the monarchs of the earth." But again, scholars say that St. Joseph exceeds the Apostles in titles and glorious offices for which he received many graces.

Likewise, comes the objection raised by the declaration of Christ Himself, who said, "There has not arisen among them that are born of women a greater than John the Baptist" (Lk 7:21). This, some may argue, may infer that St. Joseph may be equal to St. John the Baptist, but not greater. Once again, theologians and Church officials are in agreement that this is not true. Pope Benedict XIV writes that Jesus was not speaking here absolutely, but comparatively. Indeed, scholars say He was speaking of St. John the Baptist as compared to the saints and prophets of the Old Testament, and, was excluding from this association those who ought to be excluded, as in all general assertions. Thus, from this declaration, Jesus was excluding Himself and Mary, and, therefore, also St. Joseph. This is because they all belonged to a higher order than that of the Baptist. St. Jerome concurs. He states that Jesus was speaking "only of those saints of the Old Testament." Father Edward Healy Thompson discusses this issue in his book, *The Life and Glories of St. Joseph*:

> Others, indeed, and with much reason, maintain that St. John is not here compared by Jesus with all the Saints, but only with the prophets, he being, in fact, the 'Precursor Prophet'; and that it is clearly in this sense that He must be understood, would it appear

from the context in St. Matthew's Gospel, where, speaking of St. John to the multitude, Jesus asked `What did you go out into the desert to see? A prophet? Yea, I tell you, and more than a prophet;' adding afterwards, 'And if you will receive it, he is Elias that is to come'. The meaning, therefore, of what Jesus proceeded to say was that among those who were born of women there had not risen a greater prophet than John the Baptist; and he was greater in this respect, than the other prophets who beheld the Messiah in spirit and announced Him as present. The words of our Lord, as given in St. Luke's Gospel, confirm this view: `Among those that are born of women there is not a greater *prophet* than John the Baptist.' Zachary had foretold that his child should be called 'the prophet of the Highest'; and Holy Church herself styles him the greatest of the prophets, and in her hymns declares the reason, namely, that the prophets who preceded him prophesied of Jesus from afar, but John pointed him out with his finger as present, and as the Lamb of God, come to take away the sins of the world. Besides, in the very declaration which Jesus made, He expresses a limitation of John's superiority, adding, 'Yet he that is the lesser in the Kingdom of Heaven is greater that he'; by which we may understand he that is most profoundly humble; Jesus in these words alluding in a special sense to Himself, next to Mary, and then St. Joseph, who for the greatness of his humility was, with the exception of the Blessed Virgin, unsurpassed by any saint. So, too, when His disciples asked our Lord who was the greater in the Kingdom of Heaven He called unto Him a little child and, setting him in the midst of them, He said, 'Whosoever shall humble himself as this little child, he is the greater in the Kingdom of Heaven.' Therefore, since Joseph next to Mary excels in humility, it follows that he is greater than all the other saints, including the Baptist. Thus, the superiority of St. Joseph is confirmed also by these words of Christ.

Nothing in what has been said can be viewed as any derogation of the high titles and sublime sanctity of John the Baptist, who attained even to meriting the praises of God; the sole object being to remove all doubt of the preeminence of Joseph, and to prove that in his greatness and glory he must be reckoned, after Jesus and Mary, as excelling all the Saints and Angels.

As believed to have occurred before his birth in his mother's womb, there is a growing consensus among theologians that St. Joseph also received extraordinary graces after his death. Many believe that the body of St. Joseph could not have been permitted to remain on earth because of his extraordinary sanctity and station in life and, therefore, like Mary, he was assumed into heaven. This train of thought is forwarded by many great saints, such as St. Francis de Sales, a Doctor of the Church, St. Leonard of Port Maurice, and the great St. Thomas Aquinas.

The argument for such a grace is based on both theological

and historical reasons. Some writers, such as St. Thomas, argue that at the time of the Resurrection, when the bodies of many of the saints of the Old Testament appeared for 40 days in Jerusalem, it would have been impossible for God, after those 40 days, to once again reassign their bodies to the tomb. Therefore, many are in heaven, both body and soul. And if this is true, then St. Joseph would most certainly be one of them.

Likewise, it is argued that because St. Joseph held the Christ Child in his arms, Christ's Heart could not permit his foster-father to exist in heaven without engaging in the same privilege. St. Bernadine of Siena, the great lover of St. Joseph, declares his conviction that St. Joseph, because he was a member of the Holy Family, had to enjoy the same privilege as Mary in the resurrection of the body, so that in heaven they could reign together in glory according to the Apostolic rule: "As you are partakers in my sufferings, so shall you be also of the consultation" (2 Cor 1:7).

St. Francis de Sales states, "St. Joseph is, therefore, in Heaven in body and soul, of that there is no doubt," and St. Leonard of Port Maurice writes that "St. Joseph was transported in body and in soul to the empyrean by a special privilege revealed in the Proverbs which states that all of Mary's household are to be clothed with double garments." This is understood to signify the glorification of St. Joseph, both body and soul.

Some writers have even noted in their arguments on behalf of St. Joseph's assumption that a pre-figurement of such a grace was revealed through the life of the ancient Jewish patriarch, Joseph.

When about to die, Joseph, the son of Jacob, beseeched his

brethren not to leave his remains in Egypt, but to bear them to "the promised land." Moses, as Scripture notes, faithfully fulfilled Joseph's request and carried the Patriarch's relics into Palestine. Theologians say that Jesus, who so sweetly reposed upon the bosom of St. Joseph, would likewise not have left St. Joseph's body behind, but would have brought it into "the promised land" or heaven.

Finally, some note that the Blessed Virgin Mary would have interceded strongly on behalf of such a grace for St. Joseph. They say that the most pure and "holy marriage" of St. Joseph and Mary was, like St. Joseph's paternity, to endure forever and that this was ordained at the Incarnation of the Word. Thus, this alliance "in body and soul" had to endure forever. St. Augustine and other Fathers of the Church give as reason for the Assumption of Mary that it would have been indecorous for the body of one so closely united to Jesus, of whose flesh He had taken flesh, to remain the slave of death until the end of the world. And, therefore, if that is true for Mary, we are led to believe that it is also true for St. Joseph, who so faithfully served the Lord.

These scholars also note that it would be unlike God to have left St. Joseph on earth without his relics being venerated by the faithful. Indeed, history shows that God reveals the whereabouts of such precious remains through miracles. Yet, of St. Joseph nothing remains but the ring he placed on Mary at their espousal. Some theologians say it is inconceivable that St. Joseph's body would be left in the cold clasp of death for so many centuries, and that it had to be taken to heaven.

While certainly this mystery remains to be pondered, perhaps in the future we will see the Church solemnly declare—as it did with Mary—that St. Joseph was gloriously assumed into heaven, both body and soul.

CHAPTER EIGHTEEN

THE VIRTUES OF ST. JOSEPH

Contemplating that St. Joseph may have been freed from the stain of Original Sin in the womb and assumed bodily into Heaven sometime after his death is both stimulating and inspiring. As with Mary, perhaps in the future, the Church will define these mysteries as truth. However, so many extraordinary aspects of St. Joseph's life already qualify him as the greatest saint in the history of the Church that theologians are still rapt in contemplating and exploring his life. In fact, an entirely new field of study, known as "Josephology," has emerged over the last two centuries. The Josephologists meet at international conventions to discuss and examine the many mysteries and facts surrounding the life of St. Joseph. Exhaustive studies and scholarly papers are often presented at these conferences, as these devotees of St. Joseph continue to reveal to the Church how St. Joseph so greatly served God.

Indeed, St. Joseph's many titles, favors, and duties are based on his extraordinary response to the grace and will of God:

Lineage

St. Joseph was born a Jew of humble and pure lineage—a lineage that had not lost the true sense of the Messiah. Among all the monarchs of the earth that have ever lived, none have such a lineage as St. Joseph. Indeed, God Himself saw to it that St. Joseph's illustrious lineage was documented in Scripture, and was, therefore, uncontestable. The Gospel according to St. Matthew, descending from Abraham through David to Joseph, registers forty generations. In the Gospel of St. Luke, there is registered as many as seventy-four, as Joseph is traced back to Adam. In this lineage we find the great patriarchs and monarchs of the Old Testament: Abraham, Isaac, Jacob, David, and Solomon. We also find in St. Joseph's genealogy the careful fulfillment of many messianic prophecies—that Jesus should be born of the tribe of Juda, a direct descendent of David, and that He should be born of a virgin and no earthly father.

From this we see how St. Joseph's genealogy is most glorious and how God privileged him to become most worthy of whatever was to follow. For his lineage was foretold to be messianic. He was, indeed, the illustrious son of David and the "light of the patriarchs." He was "the just one."

The Jewish Patriarch Joseph Prefigured St. Joseph

Scholars say there can be no doubt that the ancient Jewish Patriarch Joseph, the son of Jacob, was designed by God to prefigure St. Joseph in Holy Scripture. This prefigurement of St. Joseph is revealed in many ways:

1. Name
2. His chastity, innocence and grace
3. In divine favors
4. Both were sons of the Patriarch Abraham
5. Both had fathers named Jacob
6. Rachel, the wife of Jacob, was buried near Bethlehem, where Joseph and Christ was born.

7. Joseph the Patriarch was clothed in a richly embroidered and rare garment. St. Joseph's soul was embroidered with equivalently unique graces.

8. The meaning of the Patriarch's vision of wheat and stars is fulfilled in the life of St. Joseph as husband of Mary and father of Christ. Therefore, he is the greatest saint to whom homage, like the stars and wheat, is to be paid.

9. Both fled Egypt.

10. Both proved heroic chastity.

11. Both received supernatural knowledge through dreams.

12. Joseph the Patriarch rises to head the house of the pharaoh, while St. Joseph rises to head God's house.

Theologians record many more examples of the prefigurement of St. Joseph in the life of Joseph, the Patriarch. Most of all, it is important to recognize the goodness and holiness of their souls.

Joseph The Carpenter

"Is this not the carpenter's son?" (Mt 13:55). The preceding verse of Scripture, through the mysterious ways of God, has led to one of the most appealing titles of the great Saint. In it, the great humility of St. Joseph is further understood. From connecting such a trade with the coming "cross" of Christ, to seeing St. Joseph's work with his hands in relationship to God the Father creating the world with "his hands," the laboring

St. Joseph's dignity has always been enhanced by his occupation.

Work, it is understood through Scripture, makes men happy on earth and St. Joseph's work is clearly found to exemplify this in a holy way. For he is portrayed as conducting his work in the spirit of faith and obedience to his loving Father in heaven. This work is then blessed by the Father to provide for the earthly needs of the Virgin Mary and Jesus.

St. Joseph, the worthy designated patron of workmen, was of nobility but accepted a profession that was hidden and toilsome. It was a position that he consecrated with his holy hands, teaching all to this day that they may obtain their "daily bread" with dignity by the sweat of their brow, and through their toil, secure heavenly salvation. Indeed, this is exactly the message Pope Pius XII sought to send when he placed the new feast of "St. Joseph the Worker" on the calendar. Likewise, Pope John Paul II writes of St. Joseph in his 1989 encyclical *Redemptoris Custos:*

> This patronage must be invoked, and it is always necessary for the Church, not only to defend it against dangers ceaselessly cropping up, but also and above all to support it in those fearful efforts at evangelizing the world, and spreading the new evangelization among nations where the Christian religion and life were formerly the most flourishing, but are now put to a difficult test....May St. Joseph become for all a singular master in the service of the saving mission of Christ that is incumbent on each and every one of us in the Church: To spouses, to parents, to those who live by the work of their hands or by any other

work, to persons called to contemplative life
as well as to those called to the apostolate.

Beloved Spouse of Mary

Scholars say a unique love existed between Joseph and Mary.
Their devotion to each other was perfect, and to this day,
serves as an example to all. In the lives of St. Joseph and
Mary there was present every supernatural and natural
element that a perfect relationship demands. Indeed, he did
not love her with his intellect and will alone, for he was a
person who reached fullness and completeness in all he did.
Passion and physical attributes were subordinated, and their
total acceptance of the primacy of the spirit ruled.

In order to be worthy of Mary, the Most Holy Trinity
endowed St. Joseph with all the qualities such a marriage
would need. Virginity was a shared promise in the marriage,
writers say, as both St. Joseph and Mary were to remain true
to their vows of purity.

As spouse of the "Mother of God," scholars say this vow of
chastity became what Joseph loved most in Mary. In her
purity, he was able to accept the intervention of the Holy
Spirit and, consequently, that the Messiah was to become
their child. Such a love, therefore, was truly divine in its
conception.   Fr. Michael O'Carrol writes about the
relationship between Mary and St. Joseph in his book,
Joseph, Son of David:

> The love between Mary and Joseph followed
> a triple channel. They sought first to attune
> their free acts to the divine rhythm in which
> they were wholly contained. In their words
> and gestures, in their mutual conduct and in

177

their final choice, they moved with a certainty of divine help and a belief in the divine pattern which was absolute. They had not the misgivings of the immature that God is indifferent to the destiny and happiness of two beings who choose each other in love. They had not the crudeness of the passionate who degrade themselves by perverting the order instituted by God, and by following impulses that drive them from His way.

Consciousness of God is not difficult for two beings who wish righteously to seek out the way of their mutual destiny. Their meeting is an act of Providence; their growth in knowledge and love needs at every stage His assistance and His protection; their exchange of free gifts, if it is to bring happiness, must touch the ultimate source of freedom which is the sovereign will of God. Realization of that truth was implicit in all that Mary and Joseph did.

Such was the greatest and most perfect marriage. It was a marriage designed to honor God and to honor marriage. Choosing the most just of men, God gave Joseph the most perfect wife who would then aid him to attain the highest level of perfection. "They were one spirit", says St. Ambrose, that possessed "one and the same heavenly divine life."

Interior Perfection

Each of the many virtues and graces of St. Joseph demand attention, but perhaps none more so than the great Saint's interior life.

Indeed, St. Joseph was, without question, a man within whom God came and dwelt. His every action can be seen as a perfect reflection of God's inspiration and guidance. Most of all, as foster-father of Christ and husband of Mary, St. Joseph came to understand that in such an important position as this, the family of all families, his perfect docility to God's guiding grace was of the utmost importance in order that the Saviour's mission be fulfilled.

According to theologians, an understandment of St. Joseph's extraordinary interior life must begin with an understandment of the man's great fidelity to grace. It is said that St. Joseph carefully and patiently listened for God's enlightment on every matter. This mean's that St. Joseph understood that God would speak to his mind, give him the strength to decide, and fortify his will to confront and avoid evil. Through this grace, St. Joseph came to trust that God was ever present in helping him to move always in the right direction.

According to scholars and to private revelation, this grace revealed itself in St. Joseph as a young man and according to some, as a child, and perhaps even in the womb. This was because God had to prepare St. Joseph for his important life, and while St. Joseph certainly was a chosen and blessed soul, his response to God's call still had to come through his own free will.

Indeed, St. Joseph was not born a saint. He had to learn to cooperate with God's graces and nurturing love. And he had to learn that fidelity to God's grace would take patience through trial and error.

The mystics reveal a gradual preparation of St. Joseph through repeated humiliations and disappointments. Over and over, St. Joseph experienced rejection, disappointment, condemnations, and, in some cases, psychological and mental abuse. But in every trial the great Saint responded in a Christ-like manner. With the humblest acceptance and steadiest perseverance, he became a mirror of patience. Through God's grace, Joseph deemed anger and rebuttal as unworthy responses.

Rather, he viewed himself as deserving of his trials and tribulations because of his own deficiencies, and repeatedly accepted the afflictions his life. Over time, he so often found himself under persecution, that he came to totally rely on God for everything. Indeed, St. Joseph realized that he was all weakness and God was all strength, that he was nothing and the Almighty was everything. Thus, he came to understand that he must turn to God for everything, big and small.

This created within his interior the perfect environment for God's grace to prepare him to head the Holy Family. St. Joseph, the littlest of men in his own eyes, evolved through God's grace into the biggest of men in God eyes.

As St. Joseph matured, his life garnished God's graces one after the other, and the molding of the "super-Saint" became perfect. Within, St. Joseph now turned to God for everything, and through his interior prayer life he became the recipient of new graces that allowed him to appreciate how God was working within him. Most of all, the love of St. Joseph began to blossom like a flower, and he, in the tradition of his lineage, began to hunger interiorly for the coming of the Messiah. This hunger for the Messiah was given to him as another grace from God to prepare him for his dual roles as husband of Mary and foster-father of Christ.

He also began to long for the day that all souls would welcome with love and open arms the fulfillment of the messianic promise, and thus, his prayers became more focused on this longing of his heart. The mystics say that it was this same great love that caused him to become very devoted to the dying in his lifetime, which is why today he is recognized as the patron of the dying and the hope of the sick.

This beautiful picture of the steady growth of St. Joseph's interior life is complex. But most of all, it is important to understand how pleasing St. Joseph's prayers were in the eyes of God and how God, in recognizing Joseph's obedience and faithfulness in the little things, came to supernaturally prepare him for the greater things. In the plan of God, St. Joseph came to know that order and love are at the heart of a holy life, and, therefore, he rejected ambition, impurity, self-pity, envy and regret.

Instead, the perfection of his interior life centered around the need for his soul to retain its peace, love, and order through the quiet of God's ways. This inner peace allowed God to come and dwell in him. St. Joseph realized that preservation and perfection of this peace would always give him the happiness and strength to survive and overcome every trial and difficulty. This inner peace also allowed him to embrace his poverty and to actually love it.

Of course, we know that there were many trials, especially in the events surrounding the Nativity and the Holy Family's exile into Egypt. But certainly, there were many more. Still, St. Joseph's interior life of grace prepared him to turn over everything to God. In his great love for God, he understood with confidence God's great love for him and that God's love was greater that any problem or trial. Prayer, Divine Prudence, and acceptance were the keys to fulfilling his mission as head of the Holy Family. And as we know, St. Joseph fulfilled this mission in life in an extraordinary way.

Most of all, it is noted how the truest measure of the great interior perfection of this soul lies in the way St. Joseph contained within himself all that God had given him. It was St. Joseph himself who kept the record of his own immense virtues sealed. His modesty and humility prevented the revelation of his perfection and, therefore, his perfection had the appearance of common life. We know of his silence from the Gospels and the accounts of the mystics. Therefore, St. Joseph's modesty of heart and purity of soul remained a mystery for centuries until God Himself decided that this great soul should be understood and treasured for who he truly was in the service of almighty God.

Father of Christ

The special vocation of St. Joseph as foster father of Christ is perhaps the pinnacle of his mission in God's service. (Note: Contemporary theologians now say that the proper title for this role of earthly father of Christ should be "adoptive father," for it implies better the responsibilities of St. Joseph.) Over the centuries, this title for St. Joseph has been much debated. For our purposes, we will merely maintain what the great 6th century theologian Origen declared: "The Holy Spirit honored him [St. Joseph] with the title 'father' because he supported the savior."

St. Joseph's unique role as foster father of Jesus must be understood and appreciated. For this role is the key to the Old Testament prophecy that the savior would come from "the root of Jesse" (Isaiah 11:1). No historical equivalent exists for the greatness and distinction afforded St. Joseph through this prophecy.

Theologians also note that if Mary's greatest title is "Mother of God," similarly, we must accept that St. Joseph's most precious title must also come from his relationship to Jesus through Mary.

St. Joseph's actions in his traditional roles are evidenced in Scripture, as he is seen moving the family, naming the Child, and providing for His family's earthly needs. But most importantly, behind all these actions must be an understanding of St. Joseph's love for Jesus. This love was a love unlike any other, for St. Joseph, who loved God so much, now understood that he could demonstrate that love in the most direct and visible way.

In his heart, there was engraved such a love for Christ, that theologians say it was not just a human love. St. Joseph was able to discern that his Son was both human and divine. This, therefore, was his God, the God he loved so much. Likewise, Joseph's heart was then filled with a holy love for Jesus—it was a love engendered by the very Presence of God. And while human fathers have a natural love for their own flesh and blood, St. Joseph's love for Jesus had to be greater because this child was, the angel told him, "begotten of the Holy Spirit" (Mt 1:20).

With this understanding comes the reality that no other saint was called to the immediate service of the Word made flesh as was St. Joseph. And, no other saint could have received the gifts St. Joseph did in this service. In his arms he held the Christ Child and before He was born he adored Him in Mary's womb. Many theologians have conjectured that God the Father Himself infused into the heart of St. Joseph His own paternal love. This contemplation, however, is one of great mystery, for from it has come many more comparisons of St. Joseph's role as Christ's earthly father with that of God the

Father. While this is perhaps unavoidable, contemporary visionaries cite the need to be cautious, for they say Mary has told them that "God the Father is unto Himself and that no man, [not even St. Joseph], should be directly compared to Him", even if the intention is good and honorable.

Still, St. Joseph's tremendous love for Christ must be seen in its full uniqueness as emanating from his intimate love for the Father and his earthly union with Christ. No saint can compare in such a manner of grace, and, therefore, it is perfectly acceptable to presume that indeed, aside from Himself, the Eternal Father willed that His Son be loved by St. Joseph in a manner without rival.

Therefore, we can safely say that St. Joseph's burning love for Jesus, as inspired and provided for by the Eternal Father, came from a heart no mere mortal could acquire, for none could be worthy. St. Joseph loved the Lord as God willed he should love Him, and it is incomprehensible to ponder to what degree this love must have been. Indeed, an ocean of graces must have been bestowed on this great Saint for this mission of love, and perhaps some day the heart of St. Joseph and its love for the Messiah will be the subject of countless works.

Joseph the Teacher

In the formation of this masterpiece that was St. Joseph's life, St. Joseph also took on the role of teacher. In his humanity, young Christ came under the influence and teaching of the Virgin Mary and St. Joseph. Beginning with the religious life, the Holy Family participated in the customs, traditions, rights and privileges of the Jewish people of that time. Along with other accepted duties, these were taught to Christ by His mother and father.

Theologians emphasize the religious knowledge that Jesus learned from St. Joseph and, therefore, how well God must have prepared St. Joseph to assume this role. It was a role that came not just from the mind but from the heart of the great Saint. The meditation of the Scriptures, along with the practices, obligations, and duties of religion, were not to be taken lightly. Therefore, we can only surmise in what innumerable ways St. Joseph influenced the maturing mind of Jesus. St. Joseph must have received great graces in this role, for his teaching had to be in reverence and adoration of the divinity of Christ. In addition to this, St. Joseph had to teach Jesus the social graces, the rules of public and private behavior, and the popular customs observed on the Sabbath and religious holidays. St. Joseph was also responsible for taking Jesus to Jerusalem on solemn feast days and for teaching Him how to read the scrolls and to participate in other religious services conducted at the Temple and synagogues.

According to theologians he functioned quite well in his role as an educator, and because of this, perhaps many of the words and deeds of the Saviour can be traced back to St. Joseph's noble effort.

Guardian

Almost all theological studies that examine the many roles of St. Joseph cite the importance of his responsibilities as the guardian and watchful defender of the Blessed Virgin Mary and the Christ Child.

Inspired by great love, with Christ's birth, the chaste St. Joseph took on the duties of a Jewish father. Beginning in Bethlehem and then forty days later at the Temple for the circumcision of Christ, every little step of the way was entrusted to the protection of St. Joseph. It is especially noted how important this role was during the departure from Bethlehem, as Herod's soldiers searched for the child. Mystics relate further accounts of how the Holy Family was divinely guided in Egypt, especially the valiant St. Joseph.

This third office of St. Joseph meant that all of the activities involving the Christ child's life were to be guarded by Him. All obligations were to be met by him, including his food and warmth from the cold at night. Thus, the protecting arms of St. Joseph provide us with a powerful model for today and his intercession for specific needs of families can be seen as most beneficial and worthy. In fact, the whole world at this time, and all the families in it, can turn to no greater a guardian than St. Joseph.

The Annunciation, The Nativity, and The Finding in the Temple

In studying the life of St. Joseph, scholars have always addressed three primary events that reflect the extraordinary attributes of St. Joseph: The Annunciation, The Nativity, and The Finding in the Temple.

The great ordeal that St. Joseph experienced during the period of the Annunciation is perhaps the single most contemplated facet of St. Joseph's life. This is because his reaction to Mary's pregnancy has stirred great debate over the essence of his thinking process, and consequently his virtues.

One thing, however, has emerged to be understood about the man. His very constitution indicated that he would remain at all times loyal to truth. And the one truth that was most evident to him was of the impeccable virtues of the virgin

Mary, his beloved spouse. Thus, the crises of the pregnancy, and how it came about, was never one of questioning the Virgin Mary's virtues.

Scholars say that it is incorrect to interpret Scriptures' words that reveal St. Joseph's decision to separate from the Virgin Mary, as reflecting any improper thought on his part concerning the conception of the pregnancy. Rather, St. Joseph was a just man and he had concluded that he must safeguard Mary's innocence. While he waited in hope, the entire situation made him feel even more unworthy of her.

Indeed, already aware of her many divine favors, theologians say that St. Joseph was true to himself and never for a moment thought that Mary's pregnancy resulted from infidelity. He knew, scholars say, "that sin was excluded."

The other extraordinary aspect of this ordeal was St. Joseph's arrival at a solution to the crisis. It was a solution based on love and faith. Fr. Michael O'Carroll explains that "he had concluded he must safeguard Mary's innocence. But as yet he took no decision. He waited in hope as did Mary. In answer to their hope came an angel from on high."

The birth of Christ again submitted Joseph to a difficult situation. Forced to travel to Bethlehem in winter conditions, the trip was grueling and dangerous. Then, not able to secure lodging, St. Joseph was forced to endure the incomprehensible thought that the Messiah, entrusted to his care, was to be born in a cave. Yet on this holy night, St. Joseph did exactly what God had planned. The circumstances of Christ's birth were powerfully orchestrated, and, fortunately, St. Joseph submitted to God's will in perfect obedience. He witnessed the birth of the Savior of the world. And although perhaps filled at first with mixed emotions, the mystics tell us that through Mary's clear and strong support, he quickly moved his attention to adoration of the Lord in the most humble of surroundings. As God planned, St. Joseph, along with Mary, were the first true worshippers of the Incarnate Word.

Finally, it is again noted how St. Joseph must have struggled in the terrifying days before finding Jesus in the Temple. The Venenrable Mary of Agreda, in her classic *Mystical City of God*, notes that St. Joseph suffered "incomparable affliction and grief," going from one place to another looking for the missing child. It is said that St. Joseph could neither eat nor sleep, and according to 17th century mystic, Jeanne Benigne Gojos, a nun of the Order of the Visitation, both the Virgin Mary and St. Joseph suffered so greatly that without God's assistance, they could not have survived because their sorrow was so overwhelming.

However, upon discovering Jesus in the Temple, their joy was immense. Most of all, St. Joseph remained silent and strong in his faith during all this. And at the Temple, Mary's words are seen to reflect a powerful statement concerning the fatherhood of St. Joseph. By Mary's saying, "Your father and I have been looking for you," (Luke 2:48) theologians say Mary's words reflect the sovereign fatherhood of St. Joseph. Says St. Augustine of Our Lady's words, "Mary made more of conjugal hierarchy than the dignity of her womb."

Again, all of his was according to Divine Will, for Scripture reveals that Jesus returned to Nazareth and "was subject to them" (Luke 2:51). Thus, St. Joseph's response was again perfect in the eyes of God. The faithful are urged to pray to him to be the guardian of their families. This protection encompasses not only physical protection, but also spiritual protection. For indeed, St. Joseph is recognized as the "terror of demons."

CHAPTER NINETEEN

ST. JOSEPH'S MANY OTHER VIRTUES

Over the centuries, theologians have written about St. Joseph's many other virtues and graces. These additional virtues include his virginal marriage, his hiddeness, his prefigurement by the Jewish Patriarch Joseph, his dignity, his Patronage of the Church, and his acknowledgment in liturgy.

The Virginal Marriage

While there have been objections based on Scripture, theologians and mystics throughout history testify on behalf of the virginal marriage of St. Joseph and the Blessed Virgin Mary. There is no need to cite the grounds of the objections. Rather, the words of St. Thomas Aquinas clearly enunciate why such a marriage existed. St. Thomas taught that the virginal marriage of Mary and Joseph was most fitting for three different reasons: first, for Christ Himself; secondly, for the sake of the Blessed Virgin Mary; and, finally, for the faithful's benefit.

Fr. Michael O'Carroll writes that the modern era holds an exaggerated emphasis on sex which makes it difficult for us to understand a marriage in which the dominant element is a spiritual union through love. However, O'Carroll notes that this is a feature of marriage only in a perfect state. Thus, says

O'Carroll, when a man and a woman decide to live together as virgins, and with the grace of God succeed in doing so, they attain perfection in the state to which God called them. We certainly can understand this in looking at the Holy Family and perhaps see it again to a degree in the early "virginal" marriage of Zelie and Louis Martin, which eventually produced so many spiritually rich blessings through their offspring.

Because of St. Joseph's admirable role in this great marriage, he is recognized as a pillar of families and the glory of domestic life.

Joseph's Hiddeness

Joseph's hiddeness has been marveled at by theologians over time. For thirty years or more, he enjoyed the greatest and highest dignity, but he refused to proclaim it openly. Fortified by grace, he was sustained by God in his roles as husband of Mary and Father of the Messiah. Like Christ's hidden life, St. Joseph's hidden life is inseparable because it totally reveals St. Joseph's perfect submission to the will of the Father. Thus, while St. Joseph is the greatest of saints after Mary, he was surpassed by many saints in spectacular achievement such as prophetic power, signs and wonders. Yet, his hiddeness triumphs over all of these as the perfect, silent path to perfection.

Joseph's Dignity

To appraise the dignity of St. Joseph, theologians say the particular excellence of the saint must be examined. According to St. Thomas Aquinas, two principles are involved. When God chooses people for a special office, he endows them with all that is needed for that office, and second, the more closely anything approaches its source, so much more does it enjoy the effects of that source. We clearly can see this in Our Lady, and experts say, in St. Joseph.

As head of the Holy Family, and through his marriage to the Virgin Mary, Pope Leo XIII says that St. Joseph approached the supereminent dignity by which the Mother of God is raised far above all of other creatures. For marriage is the closest union and relationship where each spouse mutually participates in the goods of the other. "Thus," writes Pope Leo, "if God gave St. Joseph as a spouse to the Virgin, he assuredly gave him not only a companion in life, a witness to her virginity, and the guardian of her honor, but also a share in her exalted dignity by reason of the conjugal tie."

Simply put, writes Fr. Michael O'Carroll, the marriage was made in heaven. But it was not only through the marriage to Mary that St. Joseph's dignity is understood, but also through the authority of the institution of marriage. As a consequence, the Word made flesh was obedient to St. Joseph and rendered him the honor given to any parent. Thus, to hold such a position over God Himself carried great dignity.

Finally, theologians also note St. Joseph's role in the Hypostatic Union as a key to understanding his dignity. This, they say, in comparison to that of the Angels and of St. John the Baptist, and even the Apostles, makes him surpass all these in dignity.

Not surprisingly, some have questioned whether St. Joseph could be seen as superior to the angels, who are pure spirits. But, writes St. Thomas Acquinas, since Mary in her role of Mother of God became superior to the Angels, the same also can be applied to St. Joseph. This is because the ministry of the Angels is partly the custody of men, but St. Joseph had custody of the God Man. The Angels ministered to Jesus, but Jesus obeyed St. Joseph. Therefore, writes St. Thomas, St. Joseph's dignity is of the greatest claim.

St. Joseph: Patron

The principal point in the papal teaching on St. Joseph is his Patronage of the Church. Indeed, St. Joseph is universal, and all comes under his protection. With this declaration, we come to understand and to appreciate St. Joseph's heavenly intercession as he is recognized as "the protector of the Holy Church." Fr. Michael O'Carroll enunciates this understanding:

> The intercession of the saints derives its power and efficacy from two things: the perfection of their charity in glory and the circumstances in which they acquired merit during life. Joseph's glory in heaven is pre-eminent after that of Jesus and Mary; for this glory, according to the teaching of theologians, will be in harmony with this singular vocation, the great grace he received and his lifelong fidelity to God's will. Pre-eminent accordingly is his intercession on our behalf. The circumstances of his life, in which he gained merit, as we have studied them are meaningful for every class and condition of spiritual client. Thence too arises his great success as our advocate.

In order to better understand this honor of St. Joseph, we must understand how we are to worship: the highest veneration is the homage paid to God. This is the supreme veneration, in both public and private worship. It's distinctive element is adoration, for God's holiness is absolute, as is his dignity.

The second highest form of veneration is paid to Our Lady, who because of her holiness and dignity as Mother of God, is of a singular nature. She is not adored, but she is deserving of praise, thanksgiving, and petition superior to all the other Saints. The Church extends this to her in the liturgy, the arts, and in many other ways.

Finally, to all other saints, except for St. Joseph, a form of homage is paid that is termed "Dulia." St. Joseph has the right to a veneration which, although not equal to the Virgin Mary, is markedly superior to all other saints. This is based on the following considerations:

(1) His virginal marriage to Mary
(2) His virginal Fatherhood of Christ
(3) His Leadership of the Holy Family
(4) His Patronage of the Church
(5) His place in the Hypostatic Order
(6) His eminent personal holiness

Theologians agree that the faithful are obliged to honor St. Joseph in a special way. This is because he was more meritorious and efficacious than all other saints except for the Virgin Mary. Indeed, St. Joseph is the model for all the faithful, regardless of vocation. But it is especially the working class that has been urged by the Popes to seek their inspiration and guidance in the vocation and conduct of St. Joseph.

St. Joseph in the Liturgy

The Feast of St. Joseph's patronage is celebrated by a special Mass and office. On May 8, 1621, Pope Gregory XV made St. Joseph's feast day a part of the calendar of the Universal Church. Special prayers to the saint are also part of the Liturgy. Finally, St. Pius X approved the Litany of St. Joseph for public worship on March 18, 1909.

CHAPTER TWENTY

ST. JOSEPH AND THE TRIUMPH

On April 22, 1984, after eight years of investigation and consultation with the Holy See, the revelations of the Blessed Virgin Mary to a Japanese nun named Sister Agnes Sasagawa were approved by the Bishop of the diocese.

Sister Agnes, whose left hand bore the stigmata, received three messages from Our Lady. These messages of Akita, Japan, were very similar to Our Lady's call at Fatima, Portugal, in 1917. They, too, referred to a terrible chastisement of the whole world if mankind failed to convert back to God.

But most of all, the revelations indicated that if those who respond to God's call at this time persevere in their faith, God's victory will come. It will be a victory ushered in by Mary, and it will come through the prayers of an army of souls especially dedicated to the Rosary.

While the message of Our Lady of Akita has always been understood by experts to be a direct continuation of the message of Fatima in its evangelical and prophetic content, a very special element of Akita's message has never received much attention. It is an important element, due to the great role that many visionaries say has been given to St. Joseph during our times. As at Fatima, St. Joseph was revealed at

Akita to be of great significance in the coming Triumph of the Immaculate Heart.

At Akita, an angel told Sister Agnes that regardless of the difficulties in securing the coming victory, the great patron saint of the universal Church, St. Joseph, would now assist in a mighty way:

> The more you offer this good intention [to respond to Our Lady's message], the angel told the nun, 'the more difficult and numerous will be the obstacles. But St. Joseph will protect your work.'

Marian experts say that this message given at Akita was important, for it brought to light the meaning of the great vision of St. Joseph and the Christ Child during the final apparition at Fatima. As such, it should not be taken lightly. It highlights what many experts have been saying for a while: that St. Joseph's life and significant role in the Church will be heralded by God in a special way before the Triumph of the Immaculate Heart comes into the world.

Indeed, the prophecies of St. Joseph's mighty intercession during our times are well known. The most famous claims that "the sound of victory will be near, when the faithful come to fully embrace St. Joseph."

At Fatima, God left no doubt that St. Joseph was an important part of His plan to convert the world through the Immaculate Heart of Mary. On September 13, 1917, one month before the final apparition, Our Lady told the three children:

> Let the people continue to say the Rosary every day to obtain the end of war. In the last

month, in October, I shall perform a miracle
so that all may believe in my apparitions. If
they had not taken you to the town to prison
the miracle would have been greater. St.
Joseph will come with the Baby Jesus to give
peace to the world. Our Lord will also come
to bless the people. Besides, Our Lady of the
Rosary and Our Lady of Sorrows will come.

On October 13, 1917, as the 70,000 stunned onlookers stared
in amazement at the great solar miracle in the sky, a series of
visions were given to the three children. These visions, also
seen in the sky, were described by Lucia Santos, the only
surviving visionary of Fatima, in her fourth memoir,
published in 1941:

> Here, Your Excellency, is the reason why I
> cried out to the people to look at the sun. My
> aim was not to call their attention to the sun,
> because I was not even aware of their
> presence. I was moved to do so under the
> guidance of an interior impulse.

> After Our Lady had disappeared into the
> immense distance of the firmament, we beheld
> St. Joseph with the Child Jesus and Our Lady
> robed in white with a blue mantle, beside the
> sun. St. Joseph and the Child Jesus appeared
> to bless the world, for they traced the Sign of
> the Cross with their hands. When, a little
> later, this apparition, disappeared, I saw Our
> Lord and Our Lady; it seemed to me that it
> was Our Lady of Doulours. Our Lord
> appeared to bless the world in the same
> manner as St. Joseph had done. This

apparition also vanished and I saw Our Lady once more, this time resembling Our Lady of Carmel.

In an interview with John Haffert, the co-founder of the Blue Army, Sister Lucia later emphasized exactly what the vision revealed in order to clear up conflicting accounts. In his book, *To Prevent This*, Mr. Haffert describes Lucia's recollection of the vision:

> When the children were asked about the appearance of St. Joseph just after the miracle of the sun there seemed to be a contradiction because they said he was standing and also that St. Joseph held Him in his arm. When I went to speak to Lucia 29 years later I took with me a picture I had prepared showing the Holy Child standing between St. Joseph and Our Lady. When she saw the picture, Lucia straightened in her chair, her face became animated. She exclaimed: 'It was not like that! The Child Jesus was standing elevated while the arm of St. Joseph gave the blessing.'

In his book, Mr. Haffert especially noted the Virgin Mary's words of September 1917, for in them are found, he noted, the great significance of the vision: "We recall again the words of Our Lady when she just announced that she would perform a great miracle so that all may believe. She added that she would bring St. Joseph with the Holy Child 'to bless the World and bring it peace.'"

Indeed, Mr. Haffert's observations are critical to our understanding of the great meaning behind the mystery of this vision, for he recognizes that God is not only connecting the coming of "His Peace" into the world with the Immaculate Heart of Mary, but also with her good and just husband, the perfect role model of human fatherhood and a contemplative model of the Eternal Father.

Mr. Haffert further discusses St. Joseph as a model for all mankind today. He also examines why God would make St. Joseph's presence at Fatima such a visible element in the mystery of the coming triumph:

> St. Joseph is not God-Man, nor was he immaculate. He was born in original sin like each of us. But his heart became one with the Immaculate Heart of Mary and the Sacred Heart of Jesus. He is the first example of the message which St. John Eudes heard from the Eucharistic Jesus: 'I have given you this admirable Heart of My Mother, which is but One with Mine, to be truly YOUR Heart also...so that you may adore, serve and love God with a heart worthy of His infinite Greatness.'
>
> How perfectly this was fulfilled in St. Joseph, mankind's model of union with the Sacred Hearts of Jesus and Mary! We find St. Joseph at Mary's side in all the joyful mysteries of the Rosary, a living and real example to lead us into the depths of these mysteries of God with us, through Mary.
>
> And as the scapular obtains for us the effect of Mary's presence in our lives, it does this also with St. Joseph. 'If Joseph is the father of those of who Mary is the Mother,' said the

Rev. Joseph Andres, S.J., 'he is necessarily the special father of those who wear the Scapular.' The devout Gerson (quoted by St. Alphonsus Liguori) exclaimed: 'O beautiful, amiable and adorable Trinity: Jesus, Mary and Joseph! United by such bonds of love and charity, you are truly worthy of the love and adoration of the children of God.'

And St. Joseph is more than just a model. He is truly my loving spiritual father. Like Our Lady he wants me to be plunged into the Love of Jesus. He stands ready at every moment to bless me, and to bring me the peace of which the angels sang over Bethlehem.

From these words we see that the great mystery of the Two Hearts, the Immaculate Heart of Mary and the Sacred Heart of Jesus, is critical to our understanding of what occurred at Fatima that day. This is because God is telling us that only through love, the love that the Two Hearts represents, will the world be saved at this juncture in history.

Mankind, as the great miracle of the sun symbolically foretold at Fatima on October 13, 1917, has reached the point of no return with the coming of the nuclear age, and it is only through love that it can be saved. Most notably through the great love of God for His people, but also, as the mystery of St. Joseph's presence at Fatima indicates, the love that men must have for each other.

All of this is known as the mystery of the third heart, that of St. Joseph's, which is to be now better known and understood. For St. Joseph, given as the protector of the Two Hearts in real life, is now given again by God as a protector for the whole human family. Mr. Haffert points out how we can embrace the significance of this mystery:

> At the same time a third heart emerges from the drama and light both of AKITA and Fatima. It is the chaste heart of St. Joseph. He appeared with the Holy Child in the sky of Fatima during the great miracle to bless the world and 'bring it peace.' At Akita Our Lady said that in the great battle now being waged by Satan and his legions, the apostles of the Two Hearts would be the object of their special hatred but that, 'Saint Joseph will protect your work.'

> We are stressing this at some length in these pages because very little has been said about the role of St. Joseph. Why is St. Joseph given as the protector for this apostalate to save the world from a terrible chastisement? St. Joseph was the protector of the Two Hearts in life. He was the Protector of the Immaculate Heart of Mary and to the Sacred Heart beating in Her Virginal womb...the Sacred Heart of Incarnate Love.

> Is it not fitting that now when Our Lady comes to announce the triumph of Her Immaculate Heart, which will be the triumph of the Sacred Heart of Jesus, St. Joseph again should be the Protector? And that this Saint of the interior life and of sublime confidence in God should be the one to obtain for us 'interior unity' and calm in the face of the obstacles Satan will throw up in our path?

Over and over Our Lady warned Sister Agnes of the terrible obstacle she would face in making known Her messages. But each time She would add: 'You have nothing to fear.' And over and over she was told: To overcome in this struggle, 'Achieve interior unity.' Our Lady said the same to Estelle Faguette at Pellevoisin. After telling her that she would be mocked in many ways, She said: 'Be calm.'

Now She sends St. Joseph to help the apostles of the Two Hearts achieve this peace of 'interior unity.' A man who was deeply involved in the apostolate for many years said: 'I can tell you one does not become accustomed to the attacks. It is never easy to be calm. This is a grace which we must beg Our Lady and St. Joseph to obtain for us as we sincerely try to leave all in their hands. For who is more desirous of the triumph of the Sacred Heart of Jesus than they?' We are invited to bury our afflictions and disturbances in the Hearts of Jesus and Mary. These disturbances can become aids to union with Their Hearts if we offer them with confidence.

On Sept. 21, 1974, the angel at Akita said: 'The more you offer with good intention, the more there will be difficulties and obstacles. To overcome these EXTERIOR obstacles pray with more confidence in interior unity. You will be protected...be sure.' 'Interior unity' is the calmness of spirit possessed only

by those truly united to God in faith. And this
is the special mark of St. Joseph. St. Matthew
describes him as a 'just man' (Mt 1:19) and
St. Paul tells us that a just man is one who
lives by faith (Heb 10:38).

Mr. Haffert also writes that the two hearts on the back of the
Miraculous Medal do more than just confirm the united of
hearts of Jesus and Mary. Rather, when one looks close at the
medal, it is especially important to understand the
significance of the space between the hearts. This space,
writes Haffert, is the space waiting for us to place our own
hearts, much the way St. Joseph placed his heart between the
Immaculate Heart of Mary and the Sacred Heart of Jesus.

The story of St. Joseph and the coming triumph of the
Immaculate Heart is perhaps much more profound than the
information given in this brief account. Many writers have
noted how since the 17th century, God has been gradually
revealing the life and importance of St. Joseph in many ways.

Certainly the many declarations by the Church speak for
themselves, as do his growing army of supporters throughout
the world. But other powerful accounts have surfaced over
the last two centuries from mystics and visionaries which
greatly add to the unfolding of this mystery. It is especially
noted how St. Joseph appeared with the Blessed Mother at
another Church-approved apparition, the silent apparition of
August 21, 1879, in Knock, Ireland. While this apparition
occurred almost forty years before Fatima, its significance to
the final victory must be noted.

On that rainy night, eighteen people witnessed the bright and
luminous presence of the Blessed Virgin Mary, St. Joseph,
and St. John the Evangelist, the author of the *Book of*

Revelation, over the top of the south gable at the Church in Knock.

That night Mary wore a beautiful rose, which foreshadowed her later coming at Fatima as *Our Lady of the Rosary*. Along with St. John the Evangelist, St. Joseph's presence at knock that night is believed to have been a mighty indicator of his universal patronage of the Church throughout history and especially now, as God's victory approaches in the "End Times."

Both saints, St. Joseph and St. John, were the individuals closest to Mary (with the exception of Jesus) when she was in the world. Their presence, according to scholars, represents the reverence God wishes the world to give its spiritual mother as it approached the "Fatima era" and the century of Mary—the 20th century. Most of all, it is especially noted how Ireland at that time was perhaps a microcosm of the suffering Church the world would come to know in the 20th century. Therefore, God wished the faithful to know through the Knock Apparition that Our Lady, along with St. Joseph and all of the Church Triumphant, were ready to help with all our needs and prayers.

While St. Joseph has certainly become today's patron saint of the real-estate market, God's desire for the world to now turn to this saint in a new and greater way is, according to Marian scholars, undeniable. Msgr. Joseph Cirrincione and Thomas A. Nelson published a book in 1989 titled, *St. Joseph, Fatima and Fatherhood: Reflections on the Miracle of the Sun* (TAN Books, 1989). In this book the authors advance the notion that the great "Miracle of the Sun at Fatima" on October 13, 1917, was directly related to a coming crisis surrounding fatherhood in our world, and that St. Joseph, because of his appearance at Fatima, was being given as the answer to this crisis:

> Now the pertinent question here is this: What did the Miracle of the Sun signify? Again, the first and obvious interpretation is that it was the sign promised by Our Lady that would make all believe in the children.
>
> But it was a sign so unprecedented in the history of the world, so unique, so fearful and so fraught with cosmic consequences, that one cannot help but wonder what its ADDED dimension was, what possible future events it might be foreshadowing.
>
> Taking together the two main aspects of this last Fatima apparition—(1) the peaceful scene of the Holy Family with St. Joseph and the Child Jesus standing to the left of the sun and blessing the world, and the Blessed Virgin Mary standing to the right of the sun and (2) the whirling, irregular movements of the sun toward the earth (the 'Miracle of the Sun') seen by some 70,000 spectators, causing terror in the people below (most of whom felt the End of he World had come)—we are faced with a contrast of two totally disparate elements. If the two are related, what is the common denominator? Were they sort of a positive and a negative of the same symbolic message, like the positive and negative of a photograph—with one image clear and sharp and the other blurred and indistinct? I dare say that if you were to ask five people for

their interpretation of the contrast between the scene of the Holy Family with the sun between Mary and Joseph (who held the Christ Child), where the sun was quietly in its normal place, and the great "Miracle for the Sun" in which the sun whirled wildly and out of control in the sky and seemed about to crash to the earth, you would probably get five completely different answers.

That is why, in offering my own interpretation of these two strongly contrasting scenes. I am well aware that not only is it not necessarily the true one, but that it is very possibly just one among several possible ones.

In my opinion, that which is the common denominator of the future event which both scenes foreshadow, has to do with fatherhood. And I am led to this conclusion by the simple fact that St. Joseph was holding the Child Jesus and that both were blessing the world, while Our Lady of the Rosary looked on. I see in that peaceful scene a reminder of what we pray in the Litany of St. Joseph: 'Head of the holy Family, Pray for us.'

And in the convulsions of the sun, I see an ominous foreshadowing of the consequences for the world which are sure to be felt if the true fatherhood of God and the traditional, strong role of the father of the family are rejected by mankind. Having the advantage of hindsight. I declare that such consequences have already come to pass.

Indeed, St. Joseph, the mighty protector of the universal Church, will now come to be seen as the mighty protector of the whole world. For at Fatima, God was inviting the world to take note that St. Joseph, a father unlike any other human father, is exactly who today's fathers need to identify with as their model. In a world where millions of fathers permit their children to be aborted, where divorce has became the status quo, and the family unit is in disarray, it is St. Joseph that God now gives the wold in a special way for its healing and its return to the hands of its Creator. He is the "solace of the afflicted" and the "pillar of families" and he now stands before us ready to secure all our needs and wants.

Not surprisingly, this is exactly what Pope John Paul II wanted mankind to understand in his 1989 Apostolic letter, *Redemptoris Custos*:

> On the occasion of the centenary of Pope Leo XIII's Encyclical Epistle *Quamquam Pluries*, and in line with the veneration given to Saint Joseph over the centuries, I wish to offer for your consideration, dear brothers and sisters, some reflections concerning him 'to whose custody God entrusted His most precious treasures.' I gladly fulfill this pastoral duty so that all may grow in devotion to the Patron of the Universal Church and in love for the Savior whom he served in such an exemplary manner.
>
> In this way the whole Christian people not only will turn to Saint Joseph with greater fervor and invoke his patronage with trust, but will also always keep before their eyes his

humble, mature way of serving and of 'taking part' in the plan of salvation.

I am convinced that by reflection upon the way that Mary's spouse shared in the divine mystery, the Church—on the road towards the future with all of humanity—we will be enabled to discover ever anew her own identity within this redemptive plan, which is founded on the mystery of the Incarnation.

This is precisely the mystery in which Joseph of Nazareth "shared" like no other human being except Mary, the Mother of the Incarnate Word. He shared in it with her; he was involved in the same salvific event; he was the guardian of the same love, through the power of which the eternal Father 'destined us to be his sons through Jesus Christ' (Eph 1:5).

One hundred years ago, Pope Leo XIII had already exhorted the Catholic world to pray for the protection of Saint Joseph, Patron of the whole Church. The Encyclical Epistle *Quamquam Pluries* appealed to 'Joseph's fatherly love...for the Child Jesus' and commended to him, as the provident guardian of the divine family, 'the beloved inheritance which Jesus Christ purchased by his blood.' Since that time—as I recalled at the beginning of this Exhortation—the Church has implored the protection of St. Joseph on the basis of 'that sacred bond of charity which united him to the immaculate Virgin Mother of God,' and the Church has commended to Joseph all of her cares, including those dangers which threaten the human family.

Even today we have many reasons to pray in a similar way: 'Most beloved father, dispel the evil of falsehood and sin...graciously assist us from heaven in our struggle with the powers of darkness... and just as once you saved the Child Jesus from mortal danger, so now defend God's Holy Church from the snares of her enemies and from all adversity.' Today we still have good reason to commend everyone to Saint Joseph.

It is my heartfelt wish that these reflections on the person of Saint Joseph will renew in us the prayerful devotion which my predecessor called for a century ago. Our prayers and the very person of Joseph have renewed significance for the Church in our day in light of the Third Christian Millennium.

The Second Vatican Council made all of us sensitive once again to the 'great things which God has done,' and to that 'economy of salvation' of which Saint Joseph was a special minister. Commending ourselves, then, to the protection of him to whose custody God 'entrusted His greatest and most precious treasures,' let us at the same time learn from him how to be servants of the 'economy of salvation.' May Saint Joseph become for all of us an exceptional teacher in the service of Christ's saving mission, a mission which is the responsibility of each and every member of the Church;   husbands and wives, parents, those who live by the work of their hands or by any other kind of work, those called to the contemplative life and those to the apostolate.

This just man, who bore within himself the entire heritage of the Old Covenant, was also brought into the 'beginning' of the New and Eternal Covenant in Jesus Christ. May he show us the path of this saving Covenant as we stand at the threshold of the next Millennium, in which there must be a continuation and further development of the 'fullness of time' that belongs to the ineffable mystery of the Incarnation of the Word.

May Saint Joseph obtain for the Church and for the world, as well as for each of us, the blessings of the Father, Son and the Holy Spirit.

[Given at Rome, in St. Peter's on 15 August— the Solemnity of the Assumption of the Blessed Virgin Mary—in the year 1989, the eleventh of my Pontificate.]

Joannes Paulus pp.II

CHAPTER TWENTY-ONE

PRIVATE REVELATION AND ST. JOSEPH

While theologians bemoan the fact that Scripture reveals too little of St. Joseph, we find in private revelation a portrait of this great man that seems to confirm many of the presumptions made about his life and holy mission.

Beginning around the 12th century, revelations concerning the life of St. Joseph began to appear. But it is with the 17th century revelations of Venerable Mary of Agreda and the 18th century revelations of Venerable Anne Catherine Emmerich that a complete picture of the great saint is revealed.

Mary of Agreda offers a detailed description of St. Joseph's life in her monumental four-volume work, *The Mystical City of God*:

> The most fortunate of men, St. Joseph, reached an age of 60 years and a few days. At the age of 33 he espoused the Blessed Virgin and he lived with Her a little longer than 27 years as Her husband. When St. Joseph died, She had completed the half of Her 42nd year, for She was espoused to St. Joseph at the age of 14.

Since he was chosen by God, St. Joseph was the most perfect man upon earth. His holiness, virtues, gifts, graces and infused and natural habits were made to correspond by Divine Influence with the end for which he was selected.

St. Joseph was sanctified in the womb of his mother seven months after his conception, and the leaven of sin was destroyed in him for the whole course of his life, never having felt any impure or disorderly movement.

Although he did not receive the use of his reason together with this first sanctification, which consisted principally in justification from original sin, yet his mother at the time felt a wonderful joy of the Holy Spirit. At the time when others come to the use of reason, at the age of seven years or more, St. Joseph was already a perfect man in the use of it and in Holiness.

He was of a kind disposition, loving, affable, sincere, showing inclinations not only holy, but angelic. In the virtue and perfection of chastity, St. Joseph was elevated higher than the Seraphim; for the purity, which they possessed with body, St. Joseph possessed in His earthly body and in mortal flesh.

The Blessed Virgin Mary also spoke of the intercessory power of St. Joseph with Mary of Agreda:

My Daughter although thou has described my

Spouse, St. Joseph, as the most noble among the princes and saints of heavenly Jerusalem; yet neither canst thou properly manifest his eminent sanctity, nor can any of the mortals know it fully before they arrive at the vision of the Divinity.

Then all of them will be filled with wonder and praise as the Lord will make them capable of understanding this sacrament. On the last day, when all men shall be judged, the damned will bitterly bewail their sins, which prevented them from appreciating this powerful means of their salvation, and availing themselves, as they easily could have, of this intercessor to gain the friendship of the Just Judge.

The whole human race has much undervalued the privileges and prerogatives conceded to My blessed spouse, St. Joseph, and they know not what his Intercession with God is able to do.

I assure thee, My dearest, that he is one of the greatly favored personages in the Divine Presence and his immense power to stay the arms of Divine Vengeance.

According to Mary of Agreda, "The intercession of St. Joseph is most powerful to obtain these special privileges":

> 1) For securing the grace of a happy death and protection against the demons in that hour.

2) For inspiring the demons with terror at the mere mention of the name of Joseph by his clients.
3) For attaining the virtue of purity and overcoming the sensual inclinations of the flesh.
4) For procuring powerful help to escape sin and return to friendship of God.
5) For gaining health of body and assistance in all kinds of difficulties.
6) For securing issue of children in families.
7) For increasing the love and devotion to most Holy Mary."

The Venerable Anne Catherine Emmerich also describes St. Joseph in her four-volume work, *The Life of Jesus Christ*:

> Joseph was the third of six brothers. His parents dwelt in a large mansion outside of Bethlehem. It was the ancient birthplace of David, but in Joseph's time only the principal walls were in existence. His father's name was Jacob. In front of the house was a large courtyard, or garden. In it was a stone spring-house built over a spring whose waters gushed forth out of faucets each of which represented some animal's head. The garden was enclosed by walls and surrounded by covered walks of trees and shrubbery.
>
> Joseph and his brothers occupied the last story with an aged Jew, their preceptor. The latter

occupied the highest room in the story, while the brothers slept in one chamber, their sleeping-places separated from one another by mats, which in the day time were rolled up against the wall.

Joseph was very different from his brothers, very talented, and he learned quickly but he was simple in his tastes, gentle, pious and unambitious. The other boys used to play him all kinds of tricks and knock him around at will.

They always treated him roughly, but he bore all patiently. Sometimes, when kneeling in prayer in the colonnade that ran around the courtyard, his face turned to the wall, his brothers would push him over. Once I saw one of them, when Joseph was thus praying, kick him in the back; but Joseph appeared not to notice it. The other repeated his blows, until at last Joseph fell to the ground. Then I saw that he had been absorbed in God. But he did not revenge himself; he merely turned away quietly and sought another secluded spot.

Joseph's parents were not well-satisfied with him. They would have wished him, on account of his talents, to fit himself for a position in the world. But he was too unworldly for such aims, he had no desire whatever to shine. He may have been about twelve years old when I often saw him beyond Bethlehem opposite the cribcave, praying with some very pious, old, Jewish women. They had an oratory hidden in a vault. I do not know whether these women were relatives of Joseph or not; I rather think that they were connected with Anne. Joseph often went to them in his troubles and shared their devotions. Sometimes he dwelt in their neighborhood with a master-carpenter, to whom he lent a helping hand. The carpenter taught him his trade and Joseph found his geometry of use. The hostility of his brothers at last went so far that when about eighteen, Joseph fled from his father's house by night. He worked for his living in a very poor family. Joseph lived very piously and humbly, loved and esteemed by all. At last he worked for a man in Tiberias, at which place he lived alone near the water.

Joseph's parents were long since dead, and his brothers scattered; only two of them still dwelt in Bethlehem. The paternal mansion had passed on into other hands, and the whole family had rapidly declined Joseph was deeply pious; he prayed much for the coming of the Messiah. I noticed too his great reserve in the presence of females. Shortly before his call to Jerusalem for his espousal with Mary, he entertained the idea of fitting up a more secluded oratory in his dwelling. But an angel appeared to him in prayer, and told him not to do it, that, as in ancient times the Patriarch Joseph became by God's appointment the administrator of the Egyptian granaries, so now to him was the granary of Redemption to be wedded. In his humility Joseph could not comprehend the meaning of this and so he betook himself to prayer. At last he was summoned to Jerusalem to be espoused to the Blessed Virgin.

Another 18th century nun named Maria Cecilia Baij, O.S.B., also reportedly received accounts of the life of Christ and the Holy Family. One of her revelations, however, dealt entirely with St. Joseph. In a single volume entitled, *Life of St. Joseph*, the Italian nun details the great saint's many hidden moments as well as his life and work in the Holy Family. The following excerpt highlights St. Joseph's spiritual development:

As he made his promise of perpetual virginity to God, Joseph's heart was filled with an inexpressible joy, God permitted him to feel this so that he might be assured of how pleasing this vow was to Him. He was then raised to a most lofty contemplation and his delightful ecstasy in which God manifested to him the value and merit attached to the noble virtue of chastity.

Consequently, Joseph's love and desire for a life of chastity increased continuously, and he felt consoled over having made the vow. He thanked God Who had inspired him to make it and who had so graciously accepted it. As a result, he actually seemed to be beside himself with joy.

That same night, the angel appeared again to Joseph to substantiate the fact of God's approval regarding his imitation of Mary in Her tremendous longing for the coming of the Messiah, and in Her fervent and continual supplications for it. He confirmed his belief that the arrival of the Messiah should be hastened through Mary's prayers. Joseph was advised to do the same as Mary, and, thereby, become still more pleasing to God. Upon awakening, the Saint immediately knelt down to pray for this intention, and with greater fervor than he had ever possessed before. In the temple, as he renewed these earnest petitions, his spirit was raised to a high degree of contemplation. He saw and experienced the same visions concerning the Messiah which had been granted to him earlier.

By means of the graces which God granted to him, and through the prayers of Mary on his behalf, Joseph attained such a spiritual status he no longer seemed to be a creature of this earth, but rather an angel of his paradise. His spirit was always immersed in God, his love more intense and his desires centered on pleasing God, through his activities.

While there are certainly other mystical revelations on the life of St. Joseph, perhaps a message from the Blessed Virgin to Father Steffano Gobbi on March 19, 1996, gives us a most concise and definitive glimpse of this greatest of saints. This message, and all of the 1996 messages given by Our Lady to Father Gobbi, received the Imprimatur of Cardinal Escheveria Ruiz of Ecuador. Ironically, the Imprimatur was issued on March 19, 1997, the Solemnity of St. Joseph. These messages provide us with the following insights:

Entrust yourselves to the powerful protection of my most chaste spouse, Joseph. Imitate his industrious silence, his prayer, his humility, his confidence, his work. Make your own his docile and precious collaboration with the plan of the Heavenly Father, in giving help and protection, love and support, to his divine Son Jesus.

Now that you are entering the painful and decisive times, entrust also my Movement to him. He is the protector and defender of this, my Work of love and mercy:

> —Protector and defender in the painful events that are awaiting you.

> —Protector and defender against numerous snares which in a subtle and dangerous way, my Adversary and yours is setting for you with increasing frequency.

> —Protector and defender during the moments of the great trial, which now awaits you, in the final times of the purification and the great tribulation.

As I express my gratitude to this country, for the homage of love and of prayer which I have everywhere received, with Jesus and my most chaste spouse, Joseph, I bless you in the name of the Father, and of the Son, and of the Holy Spirit.

St. Thérése of Lisieux

CHAPTER TWENTY-TWO

THE CHURCH TRIUMPHANT

The Catholic Church has declared hundreds of saints. Many of whom the faithful have never heard of and never will. Yet there will still never be too many saints. The reason—the saints are in union with God. They tell us of God and they draw us closer to God.

Even non-Catholics are irresistibly attracted towards the saints. And while this attraction may stem from curiosity, it often leads to admiration, if not imitation. For this reason, the saints are the best promoters and champions of the Church. We should not be surprised then that God would send them to Christina Gallagher, a contemporay Irish visionary and mystic, so they may be better known for their incredible assistance in our salvation.

Like many mystics, Christina's accounts of the apparitions of the saints are captivating. They are especially important because they allow us to better understand how they are constantly at work, constantly helping us by their intercession.

And that's what they do best. They intercede. They speak up for us. If we're hurting, they plead with God for spiritual medicine. If we're in danger, they call Heaven to our aid.

The saints can seek anything for us. They are our intercessors before God. All we have to do is ask for their help.

God has sent specific saints to assist Christina with her work. A representative sampling would include Saint Patrick, Saint Joseph, Padre Pio, Saint Brigid, Saint Thérèse of Lisieux, Sister Faustina, Saint John the Evangelist, Saint Anthony (who is Christina's proclaimed patron), and Saint Philomena (who is the patroness of Our Lady Queen of Peace House of Prayer). She has also seen Saints Peter and Paul. And in late 1993, she received visitations from Teresa Higginson, a 19th century English mystic who was known for the devotion to the Sacred Head, as the seat of Divine Wisdom.

Saint Patrick, the patron saint of Ireland, came to Christina on December 8, 1992, the Feast of the Immaculate Conception:

> *Saint Patrick came and I ran to him. He took me up in one hand. I could see and feel his hair and his beard. He held a lamb in his other hand. The hand I was in had his staff in it and he told me to hold it. It was wooden and curved like a snake. Then it turned to gold and looked ornate and fancy. I asked him why he asked me to hold the staff. He said that it contained the power of God. He smiled and said people once thought the staff was magic, but it contained the power of God. I touched the lamb and asked what he was doing with the lamb. He said it was the Lamb of God. Through sacrifice, he said, all the little victims were in union with the Lamb of God.*
> *Then Saint Patrick was looking at the sky and raised up the staff as a black cloud was*

whirling towards us. I asked him what it was. He said it was the darkness of death to blind God's people. But whatever he was saying to the dark cloud I did not hear. Then, I was looking at the sky spin, as if the sun was coming out. But it got so bright as the sky was still spinning and I could see the face of God Our Father, Who looked with pleasure at Saint Patrick.

Then I was asking him questions about the victim souls and I said was he one and he smiled and looked at his feet and said, 'Why do you think I walked barefoot?' I told him about how I felt and asked had he felt abandoned by God. He again smiled and said, 'Yes, but that was my glory,' that God's love and zeal were in his heart.

Then Blessed Michael came. It was to let me know he was with me. 'Saint Patrick, why are you always by the sea or water?' I then asked. He replied, 'Because that is where God first spoke to me. I love the sea.' (On the occasions when he has appeared to Christina, it has always been near water.) I asked Saint Patrick was he Irish, because his accent seemed Irish. He did not answer that but said on the 17th of March, the Irish celebrate Saint Patrick's day wherever they are. (He was joyous as he said this.) 'And others say I did not ever exist,' he went on. As he was walking along the shore of the sea on the little pebbles on the ground, how safe I felt. I could smell beautiful perfume.

(Father McGinnity describes this special experience, though different from bilocation and more than an apparition as such, as one in which the visionary is transposed from the here and now to a level of mystical reality in which sensory perception remains. The soul receives the Truth of God conveyed in an apparently natural way.)

The significance of this special apparition of St. Patrick, his intercession before God the Father on behalf of Ireland and his encouragement of Christina, the victim soul, became clearly evident when political events in Ireland quickly unfolded, showing sinister attempts to introduce abortion, the legalized practice of homosexuality, and divorce and euthanasia—all in direct opposition to God's Law.

Christina has had many apparitions such as this, but rather than describing them all, the best way to grasp these encounters is in her own words:

Q.   Tell us about the angels and saints you've seen.

A.   *The angels and saints whom I've seen are God's communicators to intercede for us to the hearts of the Blessed Mother and Jesus Christ. Our Blessed Mother and God want all people to be aware of them. They're our helpers, not our enemies or beings to be afraid of. To me, they are now very real. They're real friends, more than anyone on earth. We can trust them, whereas our friends around us can't always be trusted.*

Q.	What did Padre Pio look like? Does his face look like it does in his picture?

A.	*He had a brown gown, the same as in his picture. He was radiantly glowing with joy. I've never seen that radiance in any picture of him.*

Q.	Did Padre Pio speak to you?

A.	*Yes, Padre Pio spoke to me privately regarding somebody else. He tried to explain to me something because I really didn't understand what this particular person was going through. But, when Padre Pio came to me and spoke, he talked a lot about this person and about this person's life. After he explained all of this to me, I could understand the person's situation.*

Q.	Tell us about your apparitions of Saint Joseph?

A.	*Saint Joseph is always very kind and gentle. There's a gentleness about him like Our Blessed Mother. I see Saint Joseph, sometimes holding a lily. One night when I saw Saint Joseph bent over me in bed, I felt this deep love and peace from him. He transmitted to me an awareness of his protection and help.*

Q.	What did he look like?
A.	*He was a tall, thin, almost elderly man with white hair. He wore these garments that wrap around the body; one simple piece of cloth.*

They were the kind of clothes you wouldn't see today.

Q.   Did Saint Joseph speak to you?

A.   *He said I was to be at peace and that I wasn't to be afraid.*

Q.   Can you describe what Saint Bernadette looked like? Did she speak?

A.   *When I saw her, Saint Bernadette was looking at Our Blessed Mother. I can't exactly say her age, maybe 10 or 12. She had very little hands. She had on a brown dress and a grey head piece. She had a sallow complexion and black hair. She was so childlike and beautiful.*

Q.   How did you know who she was?

A.   *I didn't know who she was. I gave the description to somebody else and they said she was Saint Bernadette. I had heard of Lourdes, but I didn't know enough about Saint Bernadette. A priest once described her to me. He said to me one day, when I was talking about my experience, `you're another Bernadette.' He said this because he was referring to my lack of formal schooling. He thought that might be why Saint Bernadette appeared with Our Blessed Mother to me. I don't know.*

Q.   Tell us what Saint Thérèse, the Little Flower, looks like and what she has said to you.

A. *Oh, she's very gentle, very kind, very loving and the most beautiful of them all. She's the one I feel is really my closest friend. I think of them all as my friends. When I need help or even if I'm making a decision, my little friend, Saint Thérèse, the Little Flower, always seems to come to my aid.*

Q. Have you any memorable or special apparitions of her that you can share?

A. *I saw, during Mass, Saint Thérèse come first from behind the altar and then Saint Bernadette. Saint Bernadette was small. Saint Thérèse had <u>one</u> rose, huge; lemon coloured with a rim of red—extremely beautiful. They seemed to be sharing among themselves. Saint Thérèse bowed towards the priest.*

The Holy Eucharist in <u>enormous</u> light then appeared. I saw them, the Holy Souls, in a grey cloud, all raising their hands to the Holy Eucharist. Then little drops of blood began to stream down the centre of the Holy Eucharist.

The clouds began to turn from gray to white and the hands of the souls reaching from the clouds grew calm. From this, I understood these souls were raised to a higher level of Purgatory, but not fully released on this occasion.

Q. You mentioned that you saw Saint Teresa of Avila. Can you tell us about your experience with Saint Teresa of Avila?

A. *When I visited my friends in the north, who had great devotion to St. Teresa of Avila, I certainly had no intentions of praying to her in any way. I didn't want to hear anything about her. I just wanted my Little Flower, Saint Thérèse of Lisieux, my close friend. Then, it was at a Mass in this particular family's home that I saw Saint Teresa of Avila. She was looking at my spiritual director and observing every move he made. Then, she looked at me, very firmly. I left with an uncomfortable feeling about her until the second time, when I had an encounter with her. This time, she went to the lady who had devotion to her. She looked at her, smiled and came forward to me. This time, in a matter of seconds, I became aware of Saint Teresa's personality. She was so strong-minded. It was like, when she made up her mind about something, if there was a brick wall there, with her faith in God, she could walk through it. I found she was such a strong person inwardly with her faith in union with God, that nothing could stand in her way in the accomplishment of her work for God. And what was also given to me about her was that she could be this strong, and yet, so gentle. I was inwardly aware of all of this. After that, there came such a bond between us. She took my hand and placed three little roses in it. After that, to me, Saint Teresa was fine. I had no problem with her. I now really love her. And I feel I know her. Although I don't regard myself as being anything like her, I can now feel in myself a sense of her strength in God and love for God, drawing me to also be stronger. I can now recognize a little of her personality in myself.*

Q.   Are you saying that the sternness you originally perceived with Saint Teresa of Avila was because of her personality?

A.   *Yes. She had to be strong in faith and in union with God because of the work she had to do. She let nothing stand in the way of her accomplishing the work given by God.*

Q.   Can you tell us about Saint Patrick and the revelation you had of him with the House of Prayer?

A.   *Yes. It was beautiful. I could see Blessed Michael over the church. It had no roof. Then, he would go down into the church and he would come back up. As he did, I would hear the screaming of demons. I was totally aware of the religious, both inside and outside of the church. I was aware that some were spiritually dead. Then, Blessed Michael would come up with a tabernacle. He would open the tabernacle, take out the Holy Eucharist and bring it in his hand. He would then hand the tabernacle to an angel. There were a number of different angels present. They would then take different tabernacles and they would disappear. This action of Blessed Michael was repeated over and over. Each time he would go down, I would hear the screaming of devils. Then, I was wondering what this could all mean—no roof on the church. They were trapped. I told my spiritual director, but neither one of us knew what all this meant. So then, Saint Patrick came to me again. I was praying at home, I asked Saint Patrick about Blessed Michael protecting me, and about what I had seen with the church. What did that all mean? He said the church with the roof off represented the state of the Church today; that the authorities within the church were throwing away the treasures of God. Then he spoke about Blessed Michael protecting the Holy Eucharist. He said the House of Prayer was symbolic of the Church.*

Now at that time, the roof of the real House of Prayer, we were told, didn't have to come off for repair. But, two days later, I was told the roof did have to come off. Saint Patrick referred to the roof coming off the House of Prayer as being symbolic of the Church at large today and it also had to be stripped down. He then reminded me of the message I got about the Church being shaken to its very foundation. This was represented by what was actually happening to the House of Prayer. Everything had to be pulled down in it. It then had to be rewired, replumbed and receive a new roof. So, when he told me this, it was easier for me to accept the enormous suffering to be endured during the radical overhaul of the House of Prayer. Saint Patrick said man works from the bottom up.

But God doesn't. God works from the top down. So this is like the suffering that will happen, both in and out of the Church. The chastisement that will come will purify. I asked Saint Patrick, from the way he was talking, if the Church was going to disappear, the Catholic Church. He reassured me 'no,' but it will be purified and made stronger than ever and the gates of Hell will not prevail against it.

Q.   You said you have seen Bishop Fulton Sheen?

A.   *I didn't know who he was till I went to New York and I saw a picture. I said to my spiritual director, "This is the man I saw with the group that was helping Our Blessed Mother."*

Q.   I read where Sister Faustina and Saint John the Evangelist also appeared to you. Can you tell us about this?

A.   *I've seen Sister Faustina a number of times and I've seen John the Evangelist twice. On one occasion, I saw them both together during a vigil, yet, there were no words spoken. So, I asked my spiritual director, why would I be seeing Sister Faustina and John the Evangelist?*

Q.   How did you know it was Sister Faustina?
A.   *I knew from a picture that I had of Sister Faustina. Somebody sent me a picture and told me about her.*

Q.   How did you know it was John the Evangelist?

A.   *On one occasion when I saw John the Evangelist, he was called out of a crowd of different saints who accompanied Our Blessed Mother to the earth....He emerged from the crowd in this apparition and I could see him.*

Q.   Why did Sister Faustina and Saint John the Evangelist appear to you?

A.   *I later described this apparition to my spiritual director and talked to him about Sister Faustina and Saint John the Evangelist. I was trying to understand why I received an apparition of those two people without any apparent connection. It didn't seem to mean anything to me at first. So my spiritual director said to me he would think about it. So, he went away and a week later he got back to me and he said, 'Christina, did you get any enlightenment with regards to Sister Faustina and Saint John the Evangelist?' I said, 'No.' And then he said, 'It makes sense to me.' I said, 'In what way?' He said, 'Saint John the Evangelist has to do with the apocalypse or the 'end times,' as it's called in the Book of Revelation. Father McGinnity explained that the apparition means that it's the 'end times' and Saint John the Evangelist was the one who wrote about these times in the Apocalypse. That was the first time I knew he did that. He was shown with Sister Faustina as an indication that we are living in the time of Mercy which precedes the Justice of God.*

And on December 27, 1993, Saint John the Evangelist appeared during a Mass in light. He went on his knees in reverence, then stood up and took up a book. I wondered what book is this? And then it was given to me it was the Book of Life. (This is also the book Christina saw Jesus hold over Los Angeles, California, in a 1992 apparition.)

———————————

[This chapter was excerpted from the book, *The Sorrow, the Sacrifice, and the Triumph; the Apparitions, Visions and Prophecies of Christina Gallagher* by Thomas W. Petrisko].

St. John Neumann

CHAPTER TWENTY-THREE

FROM EVANGELIZATION TO SAINTHOOD

Since 1988, the Blessed Virgin Mary has been reportedly appearing to a woman named Estela Ruiz, of south Phoenix, Arizona. And like Christina Gallagher, the issue of saints and sainthood is found in the revelations.

Indeed, the Virgin Mary's many messages to Estela Ruiz can be studied and meditated on for months on end, but one thing seems clear. Her numerous words are, in essence, a call to action, strong and aggressive action, and we must consider them seriously if we are to grow in holiness.

Mary told Estela that her intention is to call the world to repentance and conversion. But a deeper consideration of the messages reveals that the Virgin expects even more. Once firmly on the path of conversion, she calls us to evangelization, and eventually to sainthood! Most importantly, all of this can be achieved by falling back on her main focus of love. For by loving oneself and one's neighbor, the desire to more closely imitate God — and then to spread His good news with others—will naturally spring forth.

Such an invitation to perfection is not new. Indeed, it is a call which the Church has sounded throughout the ages, becoming even more audible in recent years. In 1983, Cardinal

Ratzinger defined our times and the Church's mission:

> We need to overcome the anathematization of the sacred and the mystification of the profane. By its nature, Christianity is a ferment and a leaven; the sacred is not something closed and completed, but something dynamic. The priest has received the mandate: 'Go, therefore, and make disciples of all nations' (Mt 28:19).

Cardinal Ratzinger also explains what this means in today's world:

> But this dynamic of mission, this inner opening out ampleness of the Gospel, cannot be translated by formula: 'Go into the world and become the world yourselves. Go into the world and conform yourselves to its worldliness'. The contrary is true. There is God's holy mystery, the gospel grain of mustard seed, which does not identify with the world, but is destined to be the ferment for the whole world. Therefore, we ought again to find the courage to return to the sacred. The world does not need that we agree with it, but that we transform it.

Cardinal Ratzinger's statement is clear. The world will change for the better only if it is confronted with Christ's call for Christians to evangelization. Each generation has faced this challenge, and today's generation is no different, no less called.

While the horrors of today's modern world leave one feeling

overwhelmed by so much evil, in actuality they call us to new heights of sainthood. For God will not let the courageous defenders of His truth enter the battle alone.

Catholic Columnist Robert Moynihan captures this sentiment in his article "One Man Against the World" (*Inside the Vatican*, August-September 1994):

> Catholics have historically believed that God raises up saints in each age to keep the Church from being destroyed. This belief further holds that even if the Church's enemies enjoy success after success, and its defenders suffer seemingly endless humiliations and torments, the Church will always triumph over those who would destroy it—'even to the end of time....The greater the enemies, the greater the saints, and even more wondrous the victory granted by the Almighty.'

Indeed, the Church has always awaited the emergence of its next saints, individuals who seek to share and celebrate their victories in God's name.

As far back as the 5th century, Saint Augustine spoke of the great souls who would arise during the latter times. "Who are we," exclaimed the great saint, "compared to the saints and faithful of the latter times, who shall be called to resist the attacks of an enemy unchained, who we can feebly resist while he is yet in chains?"

Centuries later Saint Louis de Montfort prophesied that "the power of Mary over all devils will be particularly outstanding in the last period of time. She will extend the Kingdom of Christ over the idolaters and Moslems, and there will come a glorious era in which Mary will be the ruler and queen of human hearts."

He further explains the importance of veneration to Mary in this last period:

> The training and education of the great saints, who will appear toward the end of the world, is reserved for the Mother of God. These great saints will surpass in holiness the majority of the other saints as the cedar of Lebanon surpasses the lowly shrub. These great saints, full of grace and zeal, will be chosen in order to oppose the enemies of God who will appear everywhere. By their word and example these saints will bring the whole world to a true veneration of Mary. This will bring them many enemies, but also much blessing.

Approximately one hundred years after Saint Louis de Montfort's proclamation, the elders of the Church again noted the urgency of approaching times and issued a call for an army of saints. In 1884, the same year as Pope Leo XIII's famous vision of a coming war between God and Satan, Father P. Huchedé, a Catholic French theologian, wrote of this need:

> God, who never fails to raise up men equal to the wants of the times—apostles burning with zeal, martyrs endowed with courage, doctors whose learning and erudition vindicated Truth in all its beauty—will raise up at the critical juncture a vast number of extraordinary people, adorned with all the noble qualities and virtues of all the saints of preceding

ages.

Father Huchedé concluded that "if the Church be compared to an army drawn out in battle array, we have reason to believe that Jesus Christ, her Captain, would receive the best soldiers to withstand the most terrible shock....Not only saints, but also the angels will hasten to the standard of the cross and aid the Church in this, her great tribulation."

Saint Louis de Montfort, Saint Augustine, and Father Huchedé all foresaw our times. Saint Augustine knew that a day would come when hell would be let loose, while the Reverend Huchedé saw the approach of the times of Tribulation. And according to the Virgin Mary's messages, both visions were correct. As Mary told Estela Ruiz on December 4, 1993, "It is during these special times that Satan has unleashed all the powers of hell so that his evil may not allow God's children to be saved."

One year later, Mary explained to Estela in even greater detail what was happening:

> Satan has unleashed all the demons in hell, and I have come to help you, each and every one of you, to resist this evil which is so powerful throughout the world. You, My children, are not blind, and you can see this evil that is so evident all over. You can feel him trying to destroy you and thus overtake all whom he can. Many of you do not know how to fight him. I am here to help all those who desire to be helped, but you must open your hearts and allow me to touch them, that through My guidance and love you may turn to your God who is your salvation.

As time moves on and Satan accelerates his attacks on the world, you must know how to defend yourselves, how to be saved through our Lord, by His Mercy and goodness. If you allow Me to touch your hearts and lead you to salvation, you thus become strong of spirit and become the defenders of God's goodness and love.

God sees Satan's attacks and does not leave you and has never left you helpless. He is also around you, wanting and desiring that you turn to Him out of love. Only He can give you the strength to overcome Satan's attacks. Never has it been harder for you, My earthly children, to resist. However, Satan cannot overpower you if you have our Lord's strength in you. For that to happen, you must allow God to rule your life for He will give you strength and courage and help you go against the evil that pervades the world. Then you will become a powerful instrument of God, and you will receive salvation through your love for Him. He loves you, and He wants each one of you to return that love. Let me help you because as your heavenly Mother, I want nothing more than to lead you to Him, Who awaits. (October 1, 1994)

The Virgin's messages to Estela, as well as her work with the Ruiz family, clearly chart what awaits the world. A great victory of good over evil is in store, for even with hell unleashed, God will now bring into the world His greatest Triumph.

This coming Triumph was promised at Fatima, and has been prophesied throughout the world in modern times. Mary repeatedly tells Estela that God calls His faithful to share in this Triumph, for He is ready to fulfill the prophecies of Saint Augustine, Saint Louis De Montfort, and Reverend Huchedé. And in order to do so, He is calling for saints.

Early in her apparitions to Estela, Mary revealed this fact:

> This evening I want to remind you that if you have heard me call to you and have decided to change your lives and made a commitment to Our Lord to love Him and follow Him, you must begin to understand what changes are required from you to live up to this commandment. I want to remind you that I am calling you to sanctity. Please, my children, do not let this word scare you. These are times in the world, especially in your land, that God is last and few people are, or want to be, committed to Our Lord. Our Lord has been set aside by many, trader for other priorities that belong to the world, and God has become a stranger in your land. It is precisely for this reason that those that have heard my call can truly work to become saints. By helping me in my work to bring others to God, you can become a saint. Never has there been a greater need to work to bring my lost children of the flock.

> To be a saint, you need to be living my messages as I teach you to love. First, to guide you to love God, Our Lord, above everything else, and then to love your brothers

and sisters in the world. To become a saint, you must begin to change your priorities from desiring the world and what it offers, to desiring God and what He offers. Our Lord offers you His Kingdom and everlasting life.

When you begin to love God over all other things, you begin to free yourself from the bond that holds you to worldly things that can become your perdition. Once you are free from worldly concerns, you can begin to give yourself to the work that is waiting for you—that of loving and helping others find God in their lives. Once you find the purpose for which you were brought into this world and follow it, you are on your way to your sanctification.

The world awaits you. Begin today.
(March 17, 1990)

Two years later, Mary confirmed to Estela God's plan to raise up saints:

The world is in need of the goodness and love of God. As Mother of God, Jesus our Savior, I come to touch men's hearts so that out of those who hear me and answer, God can raise up great saints, men and women of great faith, strong in their love of God, trusting God implicitly, men and women obedient to God's commandments. These holy people will become the light of God, bringing peace and joy to all, in God's name. (March 20, 1993)

My children, I seek those who can believe this truth, even just a few. I seek those few who have opened up to this truth, those whose faith allows them to live in hope, for you are the ones whom God is seeking to raise up as great saints to lead the world to faith, hope and love. May I ask you this day where you are at, you who listen to my words? Are you the one who will lead men to faith and hope, or are you still following, seeking to find the way? (May 8, 1993)

And nine months later, Mary spelled it out even more clearly:

I as your Heavenly Mother, come to invite you, to encourage you to open your hearts to God's Spirit that He may change you from weak humans to great soldiers of His work. For it is during these times that God seeks to transform all who will allow Him into great saints.

Those who are willing to allow the Spirit of God to work in them, open your hearts that He may fill you with courage, strength and commitment. If you say 'yes' to Him, He will fill you with His Spirit and will do great things through you.

I call on all of you, my children, who have heard my voice and made changes but have gotten lukewarm in your zeal for God, to open your hearts to receive God's Spirit, that He may fill you to make you strong again. He can turn you into souls who are not afraid of the world, who God can use to bring other souls to His love. These are times that God is seeking men and women of strong commitment to His great Commandment, which is to love Him above all else, and through his love, love your brothers and sisters in the world. I come to invite you, all those who love me, to this call. Who will answer this great need? (February 5, 1994)

Sainthood! That's what it's all about. Nothing in life, Mary repeatedly explained to Estela, should be considered a higher call. And clearly, Cardinal Ratzinger, Saint Augustine, Saint Louis de Montfort and Father Huchedé were saying the same thing. We live only one life, and that life should be dedicated to striving to do God's will. For as members of the Body of Christ, each of us is called to this end.

Pope Pius XII clearly defined our times and the call to sainthood through evangelization in his 1943 encyclical, MYSTICI CORPORIS:

No one, of course, can deny that the Holy Spirit of Jesus Christ is the one source of whatever supernatural powers enter into the Church and its members. For 'the Lord will give grace and glory,' as the Psalmist says. But that men should persevere constantly in their good works, that they should advance eagerly in grace and virtue, that they should strive earnestly to reach the heights of Christian perfection, and at the same time, to the best of their power should stimulate others to attain the same goal—all this the heavenly Spirit does not will to effect unless they contribute their daily share of zealous activity. 'For divine favors are conferred not on those who sleep, but on those who watch,' as Saint Ambrose says.

Not surprisingly, by late 1994, the Virgin Mary again made this same plea for saints at Medjugorje:

> I am with you and I rejoice today because the Most High has granted me to be with you and to teach you and to guide you on the path of perfection. Little children, I wish you to be a beautiful bouquet of flowers which I wish to present to God for the day of All Saints. I invite you to open yourselves and to live, taking the saints as an example. Mother Church has chosen them, that they may be an impulse for your daily life."(October 25, 1994)

And indeed, this call is addressed to everyone, including the least of her children, those who believe themselves to be the most isolated and alone, or the least worthy of her motherly concern.

———————————

[This chapter was excerpted from the book, *For the Soul of the Family, the Apparitions of the Blessed Virgin Mary to Estela Ruiz and How One Family Came Back to God*, by Thomas W. Petrisko.]

CHAPTER TWENTY-FOUR

THE SECOND PENTECOST

The preparatory phase for the Great Jubilee must take place over the span of three years, from 1997 to 1999. This phase, says Pope John Paul II must be theological, and, therefore, Trinitarian.

The first year, 1997, was devoted to reflection on Jesus Christ, the Word of God, made man by the power of the Holy Spirit. 1998, the second of the preparatory years, was dedicated in a special way to the Holy Spirit and to His sanctifying presence within Christ's disciples. Finally, 1999, the third and final year of preparation, was dedicated to the Eternal Father and His unconditional love for every human being.

This three year preparatory period was outlined in detail in Pope John Paul II's 1994 apostolic letter, *Tertio Millenio Adveniente* [As the Third Millennium Draws Near]. Since its release, the letter has been a blueprint for many Catholic organizations to use as a guide in their preparation for the Great Jubilee.

But besides its doctrinal and evangelical elements, this apostolic letter is rich in what appears to be almost prophetic content.

The Pope's exhortations through the letter called for the faithful to be prepared for what the year 2000 is to mean for the Church and for mankind. It recognizes the challenges that the secularization of the entire world presents and that there is, especially in the West, a "crisis of civilization." This crisis, the Pope says, must be countered by a "civilization of love," founded on "universal values of peace, solidarity, justice, and liberty which find their 'full attainment'" in Christ.

But while the Holy Father's words define the times and present the solution, a closer look at this historic letter reveals a Pontiff who appears to be confident that God has a special plan for the world at this time. It is a plan of mercy and justice, and since the beginning of his Papacy the Holy Father has repeatedly spoken of the great change that will come into the world. It is a change that he has been prophesying.

Indeed, in his highly acclaimed book, *Crossing the Threshold of Hope*, Pope John Paul II clearly voices his belief that Mary's promise at Fatima of an "era of peace" will soon be fulfilled. In fact, the Pope notes that this fulfillment will come before the end of the century. The Holy Father writes that "Mary appeared to the three children at Fatima in Portugal and spoke to them words that now, at the end of this century, seem close to their fulfillment."

In *Tertio Millenio Adveniente*, the Holy Father again appears to continue this confident assertion that God is at work in the mystery of the redemption of the world which always coincides with the fullness of time—a time that is now. This subtle message to God's people presents, in reality, a serious wake-up call to those who are spiritually attuned. For God will do great things at this time and He will be in need of great cooperation from His people, especially His chosen ones.

Pope John Paul II further explains in *Tertio Millenio*

Adveniente that "one thing is certain: everyone is asked to do as much as possible to ensure that the great challenge of the year 2000 is not overlooked, for this challenge certainly involves a "special grace" of the Lord for the Church and for the whole of humanity.

How this "special grace" is to be manifested through world events is uncertain. But like Pope John Paul II's cryptic yet prophetic words, the Blessed Virgin Mary has also revealed to the visionaries of our time that God is about to bring sweeping changes into the world. These changes, emanating from His love and mercy for mankind promise a new world of peace and hope. Most of all, Mary's words announce that the Holy Spirit shall come into the world with what will be recognized as "a Second Pentecost."

This great theophany, or divine manifestation, will radically change the world according to visionaries. And, once again, this is consistent with what Pope John Paul II has been proclaiming. For since the beginning of his papacy, he has been calling for a "new springtime" in the Church.

In his second general audience of July 22, 1989, the Pope spoke of the Holy Spirit's manifestation to mankind at the First Pentecost, and how the followers of Christ experienced "a day of resurrection":

> The Pentecost event definitively leads the disciples to overcome this attitude of mistrust: the truth of the Resurrection fully pervades their minds and wins over their wills. Truly then 'out of their hearts flow rivers of living waters,' as Jesus himself had foretold in a metaphorical sense when speaking of the Holy Spirit.

Through the work of the Holy Spirit the Apostles and the disciples became an 'Easter people,' believers in and witnesses to Christ's resurrection. Without reserve, they made the truth of that decisive event their own. From the day of Pentecost they were the heralds of 'the mighty works of God' (Acts 2:11). They were made capable of it from within. The Holy Spirit effected their interior transformation by virtue of the new life that derived from Christ in his Resurrection and now infused by the new Paraclete intohis followers. We can apply to this transformation what Isaiah prophesied metaphorically: 'until the Spirit is poured upon us from on high, and the wilderness becomes a fruitful field and the fruitful field is deemed a forest' (Is 32:15). Truly on Pentecost the gospel truth is radiant with light: God 'is not the God of the dead, but of the living' (Mt 22:32), 'for all live to him' (Lk 20:38).

Today, both the Holy Father and Our Lady convey that a great change, or transformation, through the Holy Spirit will truly come again. In writing about the year 1998, the year dedicated to the Holy Spirit in his encyclical, *Tertio Millenio Adveniente*, the Holy Father stated in a very confident way his belief in what the Holy Spirit will bring to the world:

The Church cannot prepare for the 'new millennium' in any other way than in the Holy Spirit. What was accomplished by the power of the Holy Spirit in the fullness of time 'can only through the Holy Spirit's power now

emerge from the memory of the Church....'
In our own day, too, the Spirit is the principal
agent of the new evangelization....Christians
are called to prepare for the Great Jubilee of
the beginning of the Third Millennium by
renewing their hope in the definitive coming
of the Kingdom of God.

This "definitive coming of the Kingdom of God" is, without
question, a statement that many great Catholic leaders have
been repeating since the Holy Father's letter was released.
But what does it mean? Certainly, it is no secret that these
words coincide with the Holy Father's other declaration of a
"Second Pentecost" and a "New Springtime" for the Church.
But what is this great outpouring of the Holy Spirit to be?
And how will it occur?

On May 26, 1997, Father Stefano Gobbi received a message
from Our Lady about the great transformation that lies ahead
for the Church and the world. This message, along with all
the messages given to Father Gobbi by the Virgin Mary in
1996, received an Imprimatur from Cardinal Eshererria Ruiz
of Ecuador. (The Cardinal also stated unequivocally in his
letter of support that, in his opinion, this was "a message
given by Our Lady.")

In the message titled, *The Second Pentecost*, Our Lady details
the transformation to come:

> With an extraordinary cenacle and fraternity,
> you celebrate today the Solemnity of
> Pentecost. You recall the prodigious event of
> the descent of the Holy Spirit, under the form
> of tongues of fire, upon the Cenacle of
> Jerusalem, where the apostles were gathered

in prayer, with me, your heavenly Mother.
You, too, gathered today in prayer in the
spiritual cenacle of my Immaculate Heart,
prepare yourselves to received the prodigious
gift of the Second Pentecost.

—*The Second Pentecost* will come to bring
this humanity which has again become pagan
and which is living under the powerful
influence of the Evil One—back to its full
communion of life with its Lord who has
created, redeemed, and saved it. Miraculous
and spiritual tongues of fire will purify the
hearts and the souls of all, who will see
themselves in the light of God and will be
pierced by the keen sword of his divine truth.

—*The Second Pentecost* will come to lead all
the Church to the summit of her greatest
splendor. The Spirit of wisdom will lead her to
perfect fidelity to the Gospel; the Spirit of
counsel will assist her and comfort her in all
her tribulations; the Spirit of fortitude will
bring her to a daily and heroic witness to Jesus.
Above all, the Holy Spirit will communicate to
the Church the precious gift of her full unity
and of her greatest holiness. Only then will
Jesus bring into her his reign of glory.

—*The Second Pentecost* will descend into
hearts to transform them and make them
sensitive and open to love, humble and
merciful, free of all egoism and of all
wickedness. And thus it will be that the Spirit
of the Lord will transform the hearts of stone

into hearts of flesh.

—T*he Second Pentecost* will burn away with the fire of his divine love, the sins which obscure the beauty of your souls. And thus they will return to the full communion of life with God; they will be a privileged garden of his presence; and in this resplendent garden there will blossom all the virtues, cultivated with special care by me, your heavenly gardener. Thus the Holy Spirit will pour out upon the earth the gift of his divine holiness.

—T*he Second Pentecost* will descend upon all the nations which, are so divided by egoism and particular interests, by antagonisms which often set them one against the other. And thus are spread everywhere the wars and fratricidal struggles which have caused so much blood to be spilt on your streets. Then, the nations will form part of one single great family, gathered together and blessed by the presence of the Lord among you.

Today I invite you to enter into the cenacle of my Immaculate Heart, to recollect yourselves in prayer with me, your heavenly Mother. And thus together let us await the descent of the Second Pentecost, which will renew the world and change the face of the earth.

On July 5, 1997, the Virgin told Estela Ruiz of South Phoenix, Arizona, that indeed, the Holy Spirit is coming:

I tell you today that the world must be ready for the great force that is to come into the world through the Holy Spirit of God. The Holy Spirit is about to come with such power such as eye and hearts have not seen or felt. Those of you who work with Me, rejoice! For the time is here, and will grow ever stronger and more powerful, so that when you speak of God's love to others the words will come with such force that hearts and souls will listen, begin to love one another and see each other as brothers and sisters in God.

Even though Satan is still working in a powerful way, he cannot deal with the force of the Holy Spirit of God. Only those who do not want to, whose souls are so entwined with Satan will resist and may not change. But our God will give every single soul the opportunity to hear the message of love. I encourage you, My workers, to fill yourselves with God's abundant graces so that He may be more powerful in you than ever. For He is preparing a great outpouring of His Spirit upon the world. Soon the world will know that he is God, that He is truly kindness and goodness, and that He is powerful. Open you hearts and souls, My little ones, as you wait to receive Him, that He may make you His very own in His love and in His power.

And with this outpouring of the Holy Spirit will come the fulfillment of Mary's promise, the Triumph of the Immaculate Heart. It is a triumph that, according to the visionaries, will bring God's victory into the world. This victory will result in the fall of evil and the beginning of a reign of justice. Most of all, Our Lady tells us, it will bring God's peace to the world. Indeed, as Mary promised again at Medjugorje in 1984, "When the Holy Spirit comes, peace will be established" (October, 1984).

The Blessed Virgin Mary and the Christ Child

CHAPTER TWENTY-FIVE

THE TRIUMPH OF HOPE

Defining this "Second Pentecost" in theological terminology is not difficult. Many Christian writers, both Catholic and Protestant, have been writing that the age of the Holy Spirit is upon us, already invisibly transforming the world in preparation for the second coming of Christ. Now, the fullness of the Spirit will come, and a promised visible change will occur.

But the complete fulfillment of this great epiphany will be realized not just by what God will do, but especially by how mankind responds and works with God to bring change into the world. Indeed, God's gifts are to be poured out upon His people. And in their use of these gifts, the world will be renewed.

It is to be, Our Lady says, a time for the mobilization of saints. For upon receiving the gifts of the Holy Spirit, great numbers of heroic men and women will emerge to lead the world out of its darkness.

In Scripture we find an understanding of what all this means from the events of the First Pentecost. While we know that God's Spirit filled John the Baptist before his birth and that Christ's ministry was also full of the Holy Spirit, it was at Pentecost that Christ's promise was fulfilled.

In accordance with the prophecy of Joel, the Holy Spirit descended upon the Apostles and their disciples causing a permanent change in them. They received the gifts of the Spirit and the Spirit guided them to understand the full truth of Christ and how this would be communicated in the events that were to come. Now, they were to begin their mission. This meant that individually, they were to travel the paths God would show each of them to arrive at holiness and sanctity. In a collective sense, Pentecost opened the doors to the charge that Christ left them: take the Gospel to the four corners of the earth!

Now, again, this is the response God seeks from His children with the Second Pentecost. Great individual sanctity must be attained as the Holy Spirit leads the disciples of the Second Pentecost to a historic confrontation with the evil powers of our times.

Have no doubt about it, extraordinary miracles of grace are foretold and millions of conversions will take place through the "finger of God." Indeed, God's reconstructive and creative energies will produce astonishing transformations in countless souls. But much work will still be needed to bring about the complete transformation of the world as foretold with the coming Second Pentecost. An army of saints must rise up to meet the challenge of the day. These saints will be needed to help eradicate the great evil that will still exist and to secure the day for God.

This means that if we are to see the fall of the great errors of our times such as abortion, communism, organized crime, drug-trafficking, new-age paganism, pornography, liberalism, genetic engineering, and countless other horrors, it will be up to God's heroic soldiers to emerge, imbued with the gifts of the Spirit, to convert the people of the world to the truth and love found only in Jesus Christ.

We shouldn't view this as an overwhelming obstacle but as a challenge. God will pour His life and love upon the world and a new era will emerge. This is not wishful thinking if we understand that through the greatest gifts of the Spirit—faith, hope, and charity—all will be accomplished according to God's Will. Indeed, we are a people of hope and Scripture keeps this truth fresh in our minds:

> Blessed be the God and Father of our Lord Jesus Christ! By his great mercy we have been born anew to a living hope through the resurrection of Jesus Christ from the dead, and to an inheritance which is imperishable, undefiled, and unfading, kept in heaven for you, who by God's power are guarded through faith for a salvation ready to be revealed in the last time. In this you rejoice." (1 Peter 1:3-6)

Yes, we rejoice in our faith that nothing is impossible with God. God is omnipotent, and rewards hope that burns in souls. With this in mind, the words of Scripture in Romans 5 are especially relevant today: "For through the Spirit, by faith, we wait for the hope of righteousness" (Romans 5:1-2).

Indeed, in this hope we must not passively wait for the Second Pentecost, but we must ask for it with all our hearts. We must cry out, *Come Holy Spirit*, so that God may know we are ready to do our part. On May 22, 1994, the Feast of Pentecost, Father Gobbi received a message from Our Lady that revealed how the Holy Spirit will light our way and make us courageous witnesses of the Gospel in this dreadful hour of darkness:

> Today you find yourselves gathered together here, in a continuous cenacle of prayer with

your heavenly Mother, in the liturgical celebration of the Solemnity of Pentecost.

And you are repeating, with the intensity of love, the prayer which I myself have taught you, 'Come, Holy Spirit, come by means of the powerful intercession of the Immaculate Heart of Mary, your well-beloved Spouse.' *Come, Holy Spirit.*

A new and universal effusion of the Holy Spirit is necessary to arrive at the new times, so longed for. It is necessary that the Second Pentecost come quickly. It can come to pass only in the spiritual cenacle of my Immaculate Heart. For this reason, I renew today the invitation to all the Church to enter into the cenacle which the heavenly Mother has prepared for you for the final times. You are able to enter through the act of consecration to my Immaculate Heart.

I request that this consecration, asked by me with such anxious insistence, be made by the bishops, the priests, the religious and the faithful. And let it be made by all in order to shorten the time of the great trial which has now arrived.

The Holy Spirit will then bring you to an understanding of the whole and entire truth.

The Holy Spirit will cause you to understand the times through which you are living.

The Holy Spirit will be light upon your way and will make you courageous witnesses of the Gospel in the dreadful hour of the great apostasy.

The Holy Spirit will bring you to grasp that which I will make manifest to you concerning what is contained in the still sealed Book.

The Holy Spirit will give his perfect witness to the Son, by preparing hearts and souls to receive Jesus who will return to you in glory.

Come, Holy Spirit.

Come by means of the powerful intercession of my Immaculate Heart. My hour is the hour of the Holy Spirit. The triumph of my Immaculate Heart will coincide with the great prodigy of the Second Pentecost.

A new fire will come down from heaven and will purify all humanity, which has again become pagan. It will be like a judgment in miniature and each one will see himself as the light of the very Truth of God.

Thus sinners will come back to grace and holiness: those straying, to the road of righteousness; those far away, to the house of the Father; the sick, to complete healing; and the proud, the impure, the wicked collaborators with Satan will be defeated and condemned for ever.

Then my Heart-of-a-Mother will have its triumph over all humanity, which will return to a new marriage of love and of life with its Heavenly Father.

Come Holy Spirit.

Come at the voice of your well-beloved Spouse who calls You. I am the heavenly Spouse of the Holy Spirit. As through a singular design of the Father, I have become true Mother of the Son, so also have I have become true Spouse of the Holy Spirit. The Holy Spirit has given Himself to my soul by an interior and true spousal union, and of this has been born the divine fruit of the virginal conception of the Word in my most pure womb.

The Spirit cannot resist the voice of the Spouse who calls to Him. And so unite yourselves, each and all to me, my little children, in invoking today the gift of the Holy Spirit. Let your supplication become the prayer of these last times. Let you prayer be habitual, repeated frequently by you because it has been taught to you and is being passionately demanded of you by your heavenly Mother: '*Come Holy Spirit, come by means of the powerful intercession of the Immaculate Heart of Mary, your well-beloved Spouse.*'

CHAPTER TWENTY-SIX

LOOKING FOR SAINTS

In her now famous diary, Sister M. Faustina Kowalska writes of a dream she had about Saint Thérèse of the Child Jesus, better known as the "Little Flower."

Sister Faustina was a novice at the time and was going through some difficulties she did not know how to overcome. She writes that they were exterior difficulties connected with interior ones. As the situation grew more and more difficult, the holy nun attempted various novenas to different saints. But nothing worked. In fact, Sister Faustina writes that she was almost on the verge of despair, as her sufferings were so great she didn't think she could go on living.

But suddenly it occurred to her to begin a novena to Saint Thérèse, whom she had once had great devotion to before she entered the convent. So in her need she began a novena to the Little Flower with great fervor.

On the fifth day of the novena, Sister Faustina dreamed that Saint Thérèse was still living on earth and that she had come to her, concealing that she was a saint to give her comfort.

"I suffered greatly, too," Saint Thérèse told Sister Faustina in the dream. But Sister Faustina refused to believe her and rejecting her advice to trust in God more, told Saint Thérèse that it seemed like "you have not suffered at all."

Saint Thérèse assured Sister Faustina that, indeed, she had suffered. Then, she revealed to her that she was a saint and in three days, she told her, her difficulty would come to a happy conclusion.

Sister Faustina was then filled with joy and became very inquisitive about Saint Thérèse's life as a saint.

> "You are a saint?", inquired Sister Faustina.

> "Yes", said Thérèse, "I am a saint."

> "Dear, sweet Thérèse," said Sister Faustina, "tell me, shall I go to heaven?"

> "Yes", the Little Flower replied, "you will go to heaven, Sister."

> "And will I be a saint?" Faustina persisted.

> "Yes, you will be a Saint." Saint Thérèse answered again in the positive.

> "But, little Thérèse," Faustina went on, "shall I be a saint as you are, raised to the altar?"

> "Yes" replied St. Thérèse once more, "you will be a saint, just as I am."

Sister Faustina's words give us more than hope, they give a solid direction and tremendous understanding of what "saints to be" carry in their heart. Not surprisingly, they hunger for their crown and like Sister Faustina, Saint Thérèse herself spoke many times of desiring only one thing: to please God and, therefore, to be declared a saint!

"I always feel the bold confidence of becoming a great saint," wrote St. Thérèse on one occasion. On another, she stated, "God alone, content with all my weak efforts, will raise me to Himself and make me a saint!" Indeed St. Thérèse was not bashful in her words or reluctant to express her desires. She wanted to be saint and she said so quite often. "I have always wanted to be a saint," she admitted, but, "also I have always noticed that when I compared myself to the Saints, there is between them and me the same difference that exists between a mountain whose summit is lost in the clouds and the obscure grain of sand trampled underfoot by the passer-by." Instead of becoming discouraged, I said to myself, "God cannot inspire unrealizable desires. I can then, in spite of my littleness, aspire to holiness...."

Thus, through Sister Faustina's dream and Saint Thérèse's words we find that we need not shy away from seeking greatness—greatness in God. For God wants us to want this, it is not a sin of pride to desire to be a great saint.

In fact, throughout the world, God now tells His chosen ones that indeed He is looking for saints. He is looking for those who want to be saints, for truly the world is need of them. God has planted His seed in many hearts to fulfill this call. For as Our Lady tells us, with the Second Pentecost tongues of fire will again descend upon the chosen, calling them to sainthood and victory.

On June 4, 1995, Father Steffano Gobbi received a message (by interior locution) about the miracle of the descent of the Holy Spirit and how tongues of fire will come down upon

God's chosen children:

> Gathered together in an extraordinary cenacle of prayer made with me, beloved children, you are celebrating today the Solemnity of Pentecost.

> I found myself gathered together with the apostles and disciples, in the Cenacle of Jerusalem, when the miracle of the descent of the Holy Spirit took place, under the form of tongues of fire. And I saw with joy the miracle of their complete transformation. Timid and fearful as they had been, they came forth from the Cenacle courageous and intrepid witnesses of Jesus and of his Gospel.

> In the spiritual cenacle of my Immaculate Heart, the miraculous event of the Second Pentecost must now be accomplished, implored and expected by you. Again there will descend upon the Church and upon all humanity miraculous tongues of fire.

> —*Tongues of divine fire* will bring heat and life to a humanity which has now become cold from egotism and hatred, from violence and wars. Thus the parched earth will be opened to the breath of the Spirit of God, which will transform it into a new and wondrous garden in which the Most Holy Trinity will make its permanent dwelling place among you.

> —*Tongues of fire* will come down to enlighten and sanctify the Church, which is living through the dark hour of Calvary and

being stricken in her pastors, wounded in the flock, abandoned and betrayed by her own, exposed to the impetuous wind of errors, pervaded with the loss of faith and with apostasy.

The divine fire of the Holy Spirit will heal Her of every malady, will purify Her of every stain and every infidelity, will clothe Her again in new beauty, will cover Her with His splendor, in such a way that She may be able to find again all her unity and holiness, and will thus give to the world her full, universal and perfect witness to Jesus.

—*Tongues of fire* will come upon you all, my poor children, so ensnared and seduced by Satan and by all the evil spirits who, during these years, have attained their greatest triumph. And thus you will be illuminated by this divine light, and you will see your own selves in the mirror of the truth and the holiness of God. It will be like a judgement in miniature, which will open the door of your heart to receive the great gift of Divine Mercy.

And then the Holy Spirit will work the new miracle of universal transformation in the heart and the life of all: sinners will be converted; the weak will find support; the sick will receive healing; those far away will return to the house of the Father; those separated and divided will attain full unity.

In this way, the miracle for the Second

Pentecost will take place. It will come with the triumph of my Immaculate Heart in the world.

Only then will you see how the tongues of fire of the Spirit of Love will renew the whole world, which will become completely transformed by the greatest manifestation of Divine Mercy.

And so I invite you to spend this day in the Cenacle, gathered together in prayer with me, Mother of Mercy, in the hope and the trembling expectation of the Second Pentecost, now close at hand.

And with this Second Pentecost of God now calls for saints. It is a call heard everywhere, for the world must cross the threshold of hope through the efforts of the communion of saints.

Here are some of the messages that visionaries have received which note God's invitation to sainthood during our historic times.

Estela Ruiz

My Dear Children:

I rejoice with you today as you honor me in a special way. It is good to rejoice in the knowledge that God loves His children and that out of that love He gave me to you to love and cherish as My own little ones. You are indeed My little ones whom I love and as your heavenly Mother I come into this world to guide you to God's love.

Throughout the ages it has been God's will that I come into the world when My children, God's beloved ones, are in danger. It is no different now. I see many of My children in the world immersed in sin that will lead them to the loss of their souls. These are times of grave danger to the world. Many souls are being lost as they pass from this life to the next because they did not acknowledge God, and this lack of faith caused them to believe in ways that were hurtful to others and to themselves. These souls that are weak in faith are easy prey for Satan as he roams the world seeking to devour as many as it will allow him through their faithlessness.

I have come then, to call you to faith; to encourage you to believe in God and His power; to try to make you understand that it is only through God's power that you are saved. It is He Who, when you believe, can turn you into a great and powerful man or woman of God and Who can bring many others to salvation. I am here to call all those who will listen and believe to sanctity and holiness. It is those of you who have an open ear and heart that I want to guide to sanctification, to a life of holiness, to one who knows God, loves Him and serves Him. There will be very few, during these times, who will allow Me to guide them to these heights. Many will listen, make an attempt to change and then go back to the same life as before, because they expected to be repaid immediately with things of the world. These weak human beings live only for instant gratification and are weak material for holiness and sanctification.

However, there will be a few whom I will be able to guide to be true servants of God. These will be the ones who are filled with faith, who believe that God loves them, who love Him in return with great love, who never tire of doing God's work, even though their bodies may be exhausted. These will be the ones who do not expect instant gratification, but can wait to receive their reward in heaven. These will be those who carry God's love, compassion and mercy to others, at any risk— yes, even when they may be rejected.

The questions remains—where will you be? How far will you let Me guide you? Only you can answer. I love you and I thank you for listening to My words. (December 3, 1994)

My dear children:

I greet you today by telling you how much God loves you. I cannot repeat these words enough, because it is ultimately important that every soul understands this truth in order that hearts may convert. The truth of God's love for His children is the greatest truth a soul can possess. It is in believing this truth that the Holy Spirit of God can touch a soul and begin to move it first to salvation and then to sanctification. A soul must believe that it is so beloved by God that this must become the greatest, most important knowledge the soul can possess. It is this truth that moves a soul to holiness. God has loved His people, His little children throughout all generations, but it is during these special times in which you are living that He wants His love more known, more accepted, more believed. The reason is that He is calling souls to holiness.

These are times of great depression and darkness upon the world because God's children do not know of His great love. God has been pushed out of man's mind and heart and hatred and anger prevail even unto the smallest of God's creatures. Young and old, poor and rich, many, many are full of anger and hatred. So God has begun the great call to the chosen, that He may raise holy faithful believers that God is entrusting the salvation of His children on earth. This call to holiness is a formidable call, a hard but joyous journey. You who have been chosen by God can either say yes or say no, but if you say yes, God has a wonderful journey waiting.

The first step to holiness is acknowledging, believing totally in God's love for you. You, My beloved soul, must believe that He so loved you that he would become a man, come into the world and die for you. You must believe that after His death He would ascend and come back to you through His Holy Spirit to help you become a great and holy person. You must believe that he will never leave you alone, that He knows the purpose you were brought into the world for, and that He will lead you with great care to accomplish that purpose. All He asks is for you to say "yes." He will do the rest if you but have faith.

Yes, there are God's chosen walking this earth. God needs them to proclaim the message of love, be it through words or deeds of love. You, who are listening to the message, please ask yourself if it is you, and if you find that it is, then the next question is have you said yes? And if you said yes, are you allowing Him to guide you so that you may convert to His love? It is when you understand and believe in His love that you are filled and become the one who loves. Then your road to holiness and Sainthood begins!

I love you My little ones, and I thank you for listening to My words. (September 6, 1997)

Father Gobbi

The sorrow of my Heart is assuaged by you and my tears are changed into a smile, in seeing you gathered here in a continuous cenacle of prayer and fraternity, bishops and priests of my Movement, who have come from every part of Brazil.

I am always with you. I unite myself with— and give power to—your prayer. I help you to walk together in mutual love, until you become one single heart and one single soul.

I obtain for you the gift of the Holy Spirit, who descends upon this, your cenacle, as He descended upon the Cenacle of Jerusalem. It is the Holy Spirit who transforms you, who changes your heart and gives wisdom to your mind, so that you may be today a light burning on a mountaintop in these times of great darkness.

—*Spread my light* in the deep darkness which has submerged the world. It is the darkness of the denial of God; it is the darkness of the false ideologies, of materialism, of hedonism and of impurity. See how the world has again become pagan and lives under the yoke of a great slavery.

In your great nation, so ensnared by my Adversary but so loved and protected by your heavenly Mother, see how the sects, which draw so many of my children away from the true Church, are spreading more and more!

—*Spread my light*, by preaching the Gospel of Jesus with force and fidelity. His divine word must be proclaimed by you with the same clarity and simplicity with which Jesus has announced it to you. If you are faithful ministers of the Gospel, set up the strongest possible defense against the continual propagation of the sects and every form of spiritism and superstition.

—*I am glorified* by the response which I receive everywhere from many of my children, who have accepted my request to consecrate themselves to my Immaculate Heart. They are now living in my Immaculate Heart and are a gentle balm which is placed upon every wound of my great sorrow.

See how they love and glorify me. They are the littlest, the poorest, the simplest, the ones whom the world ignores, and despises.

Oh! Bring me more and more of these little children of mine, because they are for me the greatest and most precious of treasures.

—*I am glorified* by the powerful intensity of prayer which is offered to me here, in these times of aridity and great dissipation. See how the cenacles have spread everywhere, above all among children and youth, and in families.

How many families are being saved from division or have become reunited after years of separation, as a result of the great spread of family cenacles.

These are the powerful means which my Immaculate Heart gives you, to defend the Christian family from the dangers which threaten it, such as infidelity, divisions, separations, recourse to the means of preventing life and those cursed abortions which are being permitted by civil laws, but which cry for vengeance in the sight of God.

— *I am glorified* because, while neglect, disregard, indifference and tepidity toward my Son Jesus truly present in the Eucharist is spreading more and more, here the Eucharistic Jesus receives an unending homage of love, adoration, thanksgiving, and reparation.

The Eucharistic Jesus is solemnly exposed upon the altar throughout the whole day, and my little children prostate themselves in an act of loving adoration before the throne upon which reigns the Victim offered for your salvation.

How, in this place, the Heart of Jesus exults with joy, comfort, consolation, and gratitude!

—*I am glorified*, because in this country my Marian Movement of Priests has spread everywhere, as in no other part of the world.

I bless all these children of mine, who have come from even the most distant places, to take part in the three days of continuous cenacle. In them *I am glorified*!

I repeat to you again today that Brazil belongs to me, it is my property. I am Mother and Queen of Brazil and I want to bring to this great nation, where I am so much loved, implored and glorified, the gift of salvation and peace.

Thus what is taking place here becomes a sign for you which indicated to you how, in silence and hiddenness, each day I am bringing about the triumph of my Immaculate Heart in the greatest triumph of Divine Mercy upon the world.

It will soon be completely renewed by the powerful and extraordinary intervention of Her whom you invoke as your Queen and Mother of Mercy. (November 15, 1995)

Medjugorje

Dear Children!

Today I invite you to comprehend your Christian vocation. Little children, I led and am leading you through this time of grace, that you may become conscious of your Christian vocation. Holy martyrs died witnessing: *I am a Christian and love God over everything*. Little children, today also I invite you to rejoice and be joyful Christians, responsible and conscious that God called you in a special way to be joyfully extended hands toward those who do not believe, and that through the example of your life, they may receive faith and love for God. Therefore, pray, pray, pray that your heart may be open and be sensitive for the Word of God. Thank you for having responded to my call. (November 25, 1997)

Matthew Kelly

You were born to work. You were born to be saints and it is your work that will make you a saint. But until the day you die you must stand firm in your belief that it is I your God who gives life and therefore only I your God should take life.

Life is wonderful. I have sent My Son, Jesus Christ, that you may have life and have it to the fullest. Celebrate in your life and bring this message to all you meet. (May 14, 1993)

You My son have a path to follow. You don't know where the path is going, that is one of the major parts of your faith journey. You must trust in Me your Heavenly Father to guide you and show you the way. *I only enlighten you as to your direction one step at a time*. Just trust in Me and all will be well. You have nothing to fear, you have no right to fear. Your job is simply defined, but difficult. Your job is to follow.

All the best leaders in the world are not good worldly leaders because they go out on a limb on their own. They are good leaders because they are good followers. There is no need for you to be a leader. Be a follower, follow Me, and I will lead you to where it is you are destined to go.

All those around you will mistaken you for a great leader, but you and I will know that you are really a follower. Follow Me and follow

My Son Jesus Christ. Each day you must hunger for truth, justice, loyalty and love, and the many other wonderful virtues. You must hunger to be a virtuous man. You must hunger to be a Saint, after all it is for this you were born. In everything you do you must hunger to follow My way with a song of joy, peace and love in your heart. Be humble, be a follower, be Mine. (May 15, 1993)

Ask for the gift of fortitude and the Holy Spirit will fill you with the desire and the strength in each moment to do whatever it is you ought to do.

Timing is important, but timing can never be an excuse for cowardice. The time is right now for many things. The time is right now to love Me by giving Me this moment, by giving Me each moment, by doing what it is you ought to be doing when you ought to be doing it. Don't delay, don't be lazy— be a man and then be a Saint. (May 16th 1993)

God the Father: You have nothing to fear My sons and daughters, each one of you must do your own little bit. It may seem insignificant, but little by little we will win. *Evil cannot reign over good, evil cannot victor over good, you must trust in Me and do as I ask courageously.*

These end times are times for Saints. This is how it is. More than ever, there is a need for Saints and martyrs. And it is important now that people begin thinking in these terms. To be a Saint, it must be a goal that completely fills your heart and soul. No one will be a Saint without consciously trying to better themselves and be a good person.

You are presently in the end times, the next ten years will be the most important since My Son Jesus walked on the earth, his Second Coming is at hand

So I tell you be ready, follow My Son Jesus Christ. He will lead you to Me, the Father. (May 20, 1993)

My children, your individual mission is all you should concern yourselves with primarily. And what is that mission? You must be Saints!

Unless you aspire to be holy men of God then all your apostolic activities will be fruitless. You were born to be Saints. Now is the time, if you have not already, to join the road to sanctity. *If only you knew the delight I take in My Saints, just men in the middle of the world. You should never underestimate the lengths I will go to, to help one such man.*

I am the Lord your God and you are My children. Be good children, do as your Father asks and your Father will see to it that you have everything that you need.

Go now and work in My fields. Many of you

will have dual occupations. All will work in My fields, and as well as this, many of you will spread throughout the professions of the world. Many will be labourers in a more earthly sense. I tell you it is the labourer in the sun all day who raises his heart, mind, and work to My Heavenly altar that brings new meaning to the word hope.

Your hope must be simple. And your love must be simple. Work and work hard. Offer it to Me your God and that will lead you to sanctity. Hope in the future. Visualize that everyone will be offering their work to Me your Heavenly Father. How beautiful the world would be.

Pray now My Children, pray for all souls and slowly one by one gather the great harvest. Bring people back to My love. My children, enjoy the day and please labour hard in My fields. Time is scarce. (June 27, 1993)

And on this rock I will build My Church. And I have. My Church dates back to Peter. The One, Holy, Catholic, and Apostolic Church. And now the head of My Church is John Paul II, a great man.

My children, the Church will always be. I will protect My Church. I will protect the people. In fact, among you are some of the people, and they will see that the truths of the Catholic faith are delivered from these end times. They will ensure that Catholicism lives

forever and that My Church never dies.
These end times will be very difficult for the
labouers of Good. Don't despair. People will
come and go, but with them they will take
fragments of the truth. Others will come and
stay and sustain and preserve the truths of
Catholicism in their entirety.

Children you must long to be Saints. Yes, you
must long to join Me in Heaven after your life
on earth.

*It is up to you to work in My fields and My
fields are the normal streets and alleys of your
lives.*

Peter was the Rock on which I have built My
Church. Paul converted many to a love of
Me. It is here that you receive your mission.
Align yourselves with the truths of the
Catholic Church and preach to all who need to
hear My words.

Tell all to repent. Don't contain your
preaching to the converted.... (June 29, 1993)

As the years go by you will all grow in love of
Me and you will look back at your past and
see the times you have offended Me, you must
not let this play on your mind and get you
down.

I am your loving Father, I forgive and I forget.
You are human and so you cannot understand
this. *Don't limit Me, your God, to the scope*

of your intelligence.

Don't judge yourselves My children. Go to confession regularly and do small sacrifices consistently, and struggle against temptation. I am not unreasonable; this is all I ask of you.

Consider the moment at hand and the future, they are the only times that can further the glory you receive in Heaven. *Those who struggle to achieve sanctity as outlined in these messages will receive a very high degree of glory in Heaven.*

Woe to you unbelievers who disregard these messages as a young boy's mental illness, you will feel My wrath of justice on the last day. Woe to you who hear these words of Mine and carry on selfishly as though you were never exposed of My Infinite Mercy. It is a wicked society that demands a greater sign than words straight from My mouth, the Lord your God.

There is only one way to Heaven and that is through My Son Jesus. If you have read these messages you will be aware that this is not a new message, but Christ's message repeated. My children you were born to be Saints and this calls for constant change.

So today resolve that the future will be different. Then give this moment to Me; do My will. Ask yourselves: What does God want Me to do now? Then without hesitation, do it. This is how you will achieve sanctity. In the tiny moments of the day.

For very few of you have I planned large spectacular events and ways of loving Me. Most of you must learn to love Me through the ordinary events and works of each day.

Be My children. Respond to My merciful call. Do my Will. For My house has many rooms and My greatest desire is to have you living with Me in My home. (July 6, 1993)

Appreciate the gifts I have given you. My children you don't seem to understand the many great gifts I have given you.

Today reflect only on one gift. The gift of My Son, Jesus Christ. If you can grasp the significance of this gift your life will take on a whole new meaning. If you have grasped it before, recollect what you have previously discovered, and then go off again with the same zeal you did the first time you discovered it. And what is it about, this gift that is so important to all human beings? By His death He destroyed your death and by His resurrection He raised each of you to eternal life.

Supernatural outlook is what you need to appreciate this truth. There is life beyond the grave. Life isn't a game to see who can own the most, or earn the most, or have the most pleasure.

All that you are, My children, comes from Me, your Heavenly Father. I gave you all your talents and abilities. I gave you all the faculties that allow you to enjoy pleasure.

And why do you think I gave them to you? I gave them to you so that you could have eternal life. I gave them to you as means of your sanctification. My children you were born to be Saints. (July 3, 1993)

Children, Children, gather round close. My love is infinite. I am love, and I want to share it with you for eternity in Heaven.

But first you must live your lives on earth amongst the wickedness and snares of the devil. Believe in Me and he is powerless. He cannot make you do anything and I always give you the power, by grace, to conquer.

You were born to be Saints My children. You were born to be children of light. You were born to give glory and honour to Me, your God. My children, you are to be children of the truth. And I am truth. Surrender yourselves to My will. Zealously seek My will in everything you do.

You ask Me how will you know My will? The answer: pray! With prayer anything is possible. Carry My cross and you will see with clear detail My will at any given moment.

You are called to be apostles of the truth. My apostles, sent to a world so lost and confused. (July 7, 1993)

Pray for your friends and family that they might learn to see the importance of their one nature: body and soul.

My children, you must show interest and compassion for all My children. You must show concern for every soul.

The harvest is great, but the labourers are few, My children. Please gather the harvest for Me by spreading the truth. This unbelieving world is thirsty for truth but ignorant as to its source. Show people the source of all truth.

Many are caught up in self. Don't worry; they will see. In fact, the time is coming when you will all see with the eyes of your soul the truth about the way you live. And then people will hunger more than ever for the truths of the Catholic faith. Prepare yourselves My children by studying and reading. You must be able to speak of solid doctrine. You need to tell them more than the last miracle that has happened.

These happenings are to direct you back to the true faith, but instead people are becoming caught up in all these miracles. More and more people are calling for miracles: it is a wicked nation that demands a sign. Even after

I, or Mary, Mother of God, grant a sign, they still respond in the wrong way.
The only way to prepare for these end times is by personal sanctification. You must all aim to be Saints! This is My will for each and everyone of you.

You must pray, sacrifice, go to regular Confession and Communion, pray the Rosary, read the good spiritual material to develop your understanding of the basic doctrines of the Church, do charitable works, and love all souls as they were Me, the Lord your God.

This is the only preparation for the times that await at the doorstep of the world.

My son, tell the world to pray and return to the Sacraments. I am the Lord your God, I come to you out of My infinite mercy in these words, but before long I will come to you out of My infinite justice and the world will feel the wrath of My justice through natural disasters worse than those ever experienced. Now is the time to respond My children.

Seek My will in each moment and live not for pleasure in this life but in hope of Heaven.

Seek first the Kingdom of God and His justice and all else will be given in addition.

My children, spread these messages; deny no one the opportunity to hear My warning one more time.

I have spoken to this young boy, [Matthew Kelly] but I speak to you all. He is merely the instrument I have chosen to use.

These messages are to each and every one of My children throughout the world. These messages will show you how to live My will in the midst of these times. (July 7, 1993)

NOTES

INTRODUCTION
ST. JOSEPH AND THE COMING TRIUMPH OF THE SAINTS

Pope John Paul II's eulogy of Mother Teresa was a CNS story.

CHAPTER ONE
COME THE SAINTS

I referenced Pope John Paul II's book, *Crossing the Threshold of Hope*.

CHAPTER TWO
THE MAKING OF SAINTS

The quote on St. Polycarp is from *The Making of Saints* by Michael Freze S.F.O. Likewise, I used the same book for the quote on "confessors".

CHAPTER THREE
THE SCIENCE OF THE SAINTS

All of the information and quotes in this chapter are from *Quotable Saints* by Ronda de Sola (Servant

Publications, 1992), and from *The Voice of the Saints* by Francis Johnston (Tan Books and Publishers).

CHAPTER FOUR
THE FIRST SAINTS

The information in this chapter comes from many sources. Primarily used was *Church History* by Fr. John Laux (Tan Books and Publishers), *Christ The King Lord of History* by Anne W. Carroll (Tan Books and Publishers).

CHAPTERS FIVE
THE AGE OF MARTYRS

The information in this chapter comes from many sources. Primarily used was *Church History* by Fr. John Laux (Tan Books and Publishers), *Christ The King Lord of History* by Anne W. Carroll (Tan Books and Publishers).The quotations on St. Perpetua, St. Irenaus, St Polycarp, and St. Felecitas from Fr. Laux's book, *Church History*.

CHAPTER SIX
THE ADRIAN CONTROVERSY

The information in this chapter comes from many sources. Primarily used was *Church History* by Fr. John Laux (Tan Books and Publishers), *Christ The King Lord of History* by Anne W. Carroll (Tan Books and Publishers). All of the quoted material in this chapter is from Fr. Laux's book, *Church History*.

CHAPTER SEVEN
THE LAST DAYS

The information in this chapter comes from many sources. Primarily used was *Church History* by Fr. John Laux (Tan Books and Publishers), *Christ The King Lord of History* by Anne W. Carroll (Tan Books and Publishers). All of the quoted material in this chapter is from Fr. Laux's book, *Church History*.

CHAPTER EIGHT
THE CHRISTIANIZATION OF THE BARBARIANS

The information in this chapter comes from many sources. Primarily used was Church *History* by Fr. John Laux (Tan Books and Publishers), *Christ The King Lord of History* by Anne W. Carroll (Tan Books and Publishers). All of the quoted material in this chapter is from Fr. Laux's book, *Church History*.

CHAPTER NINE
A TIME FOR HEROIC ACTION

The information in this chapter comes from many sources. Primarily used was *Church History* by Fr. John Laux (Tan Books and Publishers), *Christ The King Lord of History* by Anne W. Carroll (Tan Books and Publishers). All of the quoted material in this chapter is from Fr. Laux's book, *Church History*. I also referenced the *Compact History of the Catholic Church* by Alan Schneck and *Pocket Dictionary of Saints* by John Delaney. Other references are listed in the bibliography.

CHAPTER TEN
GREAT SAINTS LEAD THE COUNTER REFORMATION

The information in this chapter comes from many sources. Primarily used was *Church History* by Fr. John Laux (Tan Books and Publishers), *Christ The King Lord of History* by Anne W. Carroll (Tan Books and Publishers). All of the quoted material in this chapter is from Fr. Laux's book, *Church History*. I also referenced the *Compact History of the Catholic Church* by Alan Schneck and *Pocket Dictionary of Saints* by John Delaney. Other references are listed in the bibliography.

CHAPTER ELEVEN
THE NEW EVANGELIZATION

The information in this chapter comes from many sources. Primarily used was *Church History* by Fr. John Laux (Tan Books and Publishers), *Christ The King Lord of History* by Anne W. Carroll (Tan Books and Publishers). All of the quoted material in this chapter is from Fr. Laux's book, *Church History*. I also referenced the *Compact History of the Catholic Church* by Alan Schneck and *Pocket Dictionary of Saints* by John Delaney. Other references are listed in the bibliography.

CHAPTER TWELVE
THE CHALLENGE OF SECULARISM

The information in this chapter comes from many sources. Primarily used was *Church History* by Fr. John Laux (Tan Books and Publishers), *Christ The King Lord of History* by Anne W. Carroll (Tan Books and Publishers). All of the quoted material in this chapter is from Fr. Laux's book, *Church History*. I also referenced the *Compact History of the Catholic Church* by Alan Schneck and *Pocket Dictionary of Saints* by John Delaney. Other references are listed in the bibliography. The Cardinal Neuman quotation is from Father John Laux's book *Church History*.

CHAPTER THIRTEEN
FROM FATIMA TO DIVINE MERCY

The information in this chapter comes from many sources. Primarily used was *Church History* by Fr. John Laux (Tan Books and Publishers), *Christ The King Lord of History* by Anne W. Carroll (Tan Books and Publishers). All of the quoted material in this chapter is from Fr. Laux's book, *Church History*. I also referenced the *Compact History of the Catholic Church* by Alan Schneck and *Pocket Dictionary of Saints* by John Delaney. Other references are listed in the bibliography.

CHAPTER FOURTEEN
SECULAR SAINTS

The saints written about in this chapter were primarily take from the book *Secular Saints* by Joan Carroll Cruz (Tan Books and Publishers 1989). John Haffert's book, *You, Too* was also heavily drawn upon.

CHAPTER FIFTEEN
THE GREAT SAINTS

The saints referenced in this chapter are primarily from *The Pocket Dictionary of Saints* by John Delaney. I also used *Little Lives of the Great Saints* by John O'Kane Murray.

CHAPTER SIXTEEN
ST. JOSEPH, THE GREATEST OF ALL THE SAINTS

Many books were referenced regarding the life of St. Joseph. I placed emphasis on Michael O'Carroll's *Joseph, Son of David*. The quote by St. Teresa of Avila is from Fr. Michael O'Carrol's book *Joseph, Son of David*.

CHAPTER SEVENTEEN
THE SPECIAL GRACES GIVEN ST. JOSEPH

Many books were referenced regarding the life of St. Joseph. I placed emphasis on Michael O'Carroll's *Joseph, Son of David*.

CHAPTER EIGHTEEN
THE VIRTUES OF ST. JOSEPH

Many books were referenced regarding the life of St. Joseph. I placed emphasis on Michael O'Carroll's *Joseph, Son of David*.

CHAPTER NINETEEN
ST. JOSEPH'S MANY OTHER VIRTUES

Many books were referenced regarding the life of St. Joseph. I placed emphasis on Michael O'Carroll's *Joseph, Son of David*.

CHAPTER TWENTY
ST. JOSEPH AND THE TRIUMPH

The quote of Sister Agnes Sasagawa is from the book *Akita, The Tears and Message of Mary* by Fr. John Yasuda. Mary's message at Fatima is from John Haffert's book, *Her Own Words to the Nuclear Age.* I also quoted Hafford's book *To Prevent This* throughout this chapter. Highly recommended and quoted is *St. Joseph, Fatima, and Fatherhood* by Msgr. Joseph Cirrincione and Thomas A. Nelson (Tan Books and Publishers).

CHAPTER TWENTY-ONE
PRIVATE REVELATION AND ST. JOSEPH

I quoted *The Mystical City of God* by Mary of Agreda (Tan Books and Publishers). I also quoted Sister Maria Cecelia Baij, OSB's book, *Life of St. Joseph* (published by the 101 Foundation and is highly recommended). Fr. Gobbi's message and all his messages in this chapter and throughout this book are from the book, *To The Priest's Our Beloved Sons.* This book is published by the Marian Movement of Priests and is quoted with permission. All of Fr. Gobbi's messages in this book are used with the permission of the Marian Movement of Priests.

CHAPTER TWENTY-TWO
THE CHURCH TRIUMPHANT

This chapter is excerpted from my book *The Sorrow, Sacrifice, and the Triumph, The Apparitions, Visions, and Prophecies of Christina Gallagher* (Simon and Schuster, NY, NY).

CHAPTER TWENTY-THREE
FROM EVANGELIZATION TO SAINTHOOD

This chapter is excerpted from my book *For the Soul of the Family, the Story of* the *Apparitions of the Blessed Virgin Mary to Estela Ruiz and How One Family Came Back to God* (Queenship Publishing 1996).

CHAPTER TWENTY-FOUR
THE SECOND PENTECOST

Father Gobbi's messages from his book *To the Priests, Our Lady's Beloved Sons*. It was used with permission of the Marian Movement of Priests.

CHAPTER TWENTY-FIVE
THE TRIUMPH OF HOPE

Father Gobbi's messages from his book *To the Priests, Our Lady's Beloved Sons*. It was used with permission of the Marian Movement of Priests.

CHAPTER TWENTY-SIX
LOOKING FOR SAINTS

Sister Faustina Kowalska's dream is from the book *Divine Mercy in My Soul* by Sister M. Faustina Kowalska (The Diary of Sister M. Faustina Kowalska), published by Marian Press, Stockbridge, Massachusetts (1987). Father Gobbi's Messages is from his book *To the Priests, Our Lady's Beloved Sons*. It was used with permission of the Marian Movement of Priests. Estela Ruiz's messages are from the book *Our Lady of the Americas* (published by the

Pittsburgh Center for Peace). The message of Our Lady of Medjugorje is from Sister Emmanuel's monthly fax from the village of Medjugorje. (The Medjugorje messages are released on the 25th of each month and are public messages.) Matthew Kelly's messages come from his book *Words from God* (published by the 101 Foundation).

SELECTED BIBLIOGRAPHY

Agreda, Venerable Mary of. *The Mystical City of God.* Rockford, Illinois: TAN Books and Publishers, Inc., 1978.

----. "As the Third Millennium Draws Near" in *Inside the Vatican.* New Hope, Kentucky: St. Porres Lay Dominican Community Print Shop, January, 1995.

Avila, St. Teresa of. *Interior Castle.* New York: Bantam Doubleday Dell Publishing Group, Inc., 1989

Ball, Ann. *Modern Saints Their Lives and Faces.* Rockford, Illinois: TAN Books and Publishers, Inc., 1983.

Baij, Maria Cecilia, O.S.B. *The Life of Saint Joseph.* Asbury, New Jersey: 101 Foundation, Inc., 1996.

Beevors, John. *St. Joan of Arc.* Rockford, Illinois: TAN Books and publishers, Inc., 1981.

Bergeron, Henri-Paul, C.S.C. *Brother Andre The Wonder Man of Mount Royal.* Montreal, Canada: Saint Joseph's Oratory, 1988.

Binet, Pere. *The Divine Favors Granted to St. Joseph.* Rockford, Illinois: TAN Books and Publishers, Inc., 1983.

Bokenkotter, Thomas. *A Concise History of the Catholic Church* (Revised Edition). New York: Bantam Doubleday Dell Publishing Co., 1979.

Carroll, Anne W. *Christ the King Lord of History*. Rockford, Illinois: TAN Books and publishers, Inc., 1994.

Chervin, Ronda De Sola. *Quotable Saints*. Ann Arbor, Michigan: Servant Publications, 1992.

Cirrincione, Msgr. Joseph A. *Fatima's Message for Our Times*. Rockford, Illinois: TAN Books and Publishers, Inc., 1990.

Cirrincione, Msgr. Joseph A. with Thomas A. Nelson. *St. Joseph, Fatima and Fatherhood Reflections on the Miracle of the Sun*. Rockford, Illinois: TAN Books and Publishers, Inc. 1989.

Cirrincione, Msgr. Joseph A. with Thomas A. Nelson. *The Forgotten Secret of Fatima and the Silent Apostolate*. Rockford, Illinois: TAN Books and Publishers, Inc., 1988.
Connell, Janice T. *The Triumph of the Immaculate Heart*. Santa Barbara, California: Queenship Publishing Company, 1983.

Croiset, Fr. John, S.J. *The Devotion to the Sacred Heart of Jesus*. Rockford, Illinois: TAN Books and Publishers, Inc. 1988.

Cruz, Joan Carroll. *Secular Saints*. Rockford, Illinois: TAN Books and Publishers, Inc., 1989.

De Domenico, Dominic, O.P. *True Devotion to St. Joseph and the Church*. New Hope, Kentucky: St. Gabriel Press.

dè Liguori, St. Alphonsus. *Victories of the Martyrs.* Brooklyn, New York: Redemptorist Fathers, 1954.

de Monfort, St. Louis Marie. *God Alone The Collected Writings o St. Louis Marie De Monfort.* Bay Shore, New York: Montfort Publishing, 1987.

Deiss, Lucien. *Joseph, Mary, Jesus.* Collegeville, Minnesota: The Liturgical Press, 1996.

Delaney, John J. *Pocket Dictionary of Saints.* (Abridged Edition). New York: Bantam Doubleday Dell Publishing Group, Inc., 1980.

----. *Dives en Misericordia* (Encyclical Letter). Boston, Massachusetts: Daughters of St. Paul.

Doze, Andrew. *St. Joseph Shadow of the Father.* Staten Island, New York: Alba House, 1992.

Filas, F.L., S.J. *The Man Nearest to Christ Nature and Historic Development of the Devotion to St. Joseph.* Milwaukee, Wisconsin: The Bruce Publishing Company, 1944.

Freze, Michael, S.F.O. *The Making of Saints.* Huntington, Indiana: Our Sunday Visitor Publishing Division, 1991.

Gibbons, James Cardinal. *The Faith of Our Fathers.* Rockford, Illinois: TAN Books and Publishers, Inc., 1980.

Gobbi, Don Stefano. *To the Priests Our Lady's Beloved Son's* (Supplements - 1993, 1994) St. Francis, Maine: National Headquarters of the Marian Movement of Priests in the United States of America, 1988.

Green, Julien. *God's Fool The Life and Time of Francis of Assisi*. San Francisco, California: Harper & Row, Publishers, Inc., 1985.

Haffert, John M. *Finally...Russia*. Asbury, New Jersey: 101 Foundation, Inc., 1993.

Haffert, John M. *Her Own Words to the Nuclear Age*. Asbury, New Jersey: 101 Foundation, Inc., 1993.

Harris, Marquerite Tjader (editor), et. al. *Birgitta of Sweden -- Life and Select Revelations*. Mahwah, New Jersey: Paulist Press. 1990.

Hughes, John Jay. *Pontiffs Popes Who Shaped History*. Huntington, Indiana: Our Sunday Visitor Publishing Division, Our Sunday Visitor, Inc., 1994.

John Paul II, Pope. *Crossing the Threshold of Hope*. New York: Alfred A. Knopf, 1994.

John Paul II, Pope. *The Spirit Giver of Life and Love A Catechesis on the Creed* (Volume Three). Boston, Massachusetts: Pauline Books & Media, 1996.

Johnston, Francis W. (editor) *The Voice of the Saints*. Rockford, Illinois: TAN Books and Publishers, Inc., 1986.

Joseph, Aaron, *In the Spirit of St. Joseph*. Enfield, Connecticut: St. Joseph's Place, 1997.

Kelly, Matthew. *Words from God*. Batesman Bay N.S.W., Australia: Matthew Kelly, 1993.

Kondor, Fr. Louis. SVD. (editor) *Fatima in Lucia' Own Words*. Still River, Massachusetts: Marian Helpers, 1991.

Kosicki, George W., C.S.B. *Special Urgency of Mercy: Why Sister Faustina?* Steubenville, Ohio: Franciscan University Press, 1990

Kowalska, Sister M. Faustina. *Divine Mercy in My Soul.* (The Diary of Sister M. Faustina Kowalska) Stockbridge, Massachusetts: Marian Press, 1987.

Kunzli, Josef (editor), *The Message of the Lady of all Nations.* Jestetten, West Germany: Mirriam-Verlag, 1987.

LaFreniere, Bernard, C.S.C. *Brother Andre According to Witnesses.* Montreal, Canada. St. Joseph's Oratory, 1990.

Laux, Fr. John, M.A. *Church History.* Rockford, Illinois: TAN Books and Publishers, Inc., 1989.

Lisieux, Saint Thérèse of. *The autobiography of Saint Therese of Lisieux.* New York: Image Books - Doubleday, 1989.

----. *Lives of the Saints.* New York: Catholic Book Publishing Co., 1989..
Lovasik, Rev. Lawrence G.. S.V.D. *Saint Joseph Church History.* New York: Catholic Book Publishing Co., 1990.

Martin, Antonio Royo, O.P. *The Great Unknown The Holy Ghost and His Gifts.* New York: Western Hemisphere Cultural Society, 1991.

Martin, Ralph. *The Catholic Church at the End of an Age.* San Francisco, California: Ignatius Press, 1994.

----. *Messages of Love The Mother of the Savior Speaks to the World from Naju, Korea.* Gresham, Oregon: Mary's Touch by Mail, 1996.

Murray, John O'Kane, M.A. *Little Lives of the Great Saints*. Rockford, Illinois: TAN Books and Publishers, Inc., 1985.

O'Carroll, Michael, C.S.Sp. *Joseph, Son of David*. Dublin, Ireland: Gill and Son, Ltd., 1963

Parente, Fr. Pascal P. *Beyond Space*. Rockford, Illinois: TAN Books and Publishers, Inc., 1973.

Patrignani, Father, S.J. *A Manual of Practical Devotion to St. Joseph*. Rockford, Illinois: TAN Books and Publishers, Inc., 1982.

Pelletier, Joseph A., A.A. *The Sun Danced at Fatima*. Garden City, New York: Image Books, 1983.

Petrisko, Thomas W. *In God's Hands*. McKees Rocks, Pennsylvania: St. Andrew's Productions, 1997.

Piat, Fr. Stephane-Joseph, O.F.M. *The Story of a Family The Home of St. Thérèse of Lisieux*. Rockford, Illinois, TAN Books and Publishers, Inc. 1994.

Ruffin, C. Bernard. *The Twelve The Lives of the Apostles After Calvary*. Huntington, Indiana: Our Sunday Visitor, Inc., 1984.

Rutler, George William. *A Crisis of Saints*. San Francisco, California: Ignatius Press, 1995.

Schreck, Alan. *The Compact History of the Catholic Church*. Ann Arbor, Michigan: Servant Books, 1987.

Schmoger, Carle., C.SS.R. (editor) *The Life of Jesus Christ and Biblical Revelations From the Visions of the Venerable Anne Catherine Emmerich as recorded by the Journals of*

Clemens Brentano - Volume 1 (4 Volumes). Rockford, Illinois, TAN Books and Publishers, Inc., 1979.

Sharkey, Don. *The Woman Shall Conquer.* Libertyville, Illinois: Prow/Franciscan Marytown Press (fourth Printing by AMI Press, Washington, New Jersey), 1976.

Smolenski, Rev. Stanley. "St. Joseph's Place in the third millennium" in *Homiletic & Pastoral Review.* San Francisco, California: St. Ignatius Press, Aug-Sept., 1997.

Stein, Susan T. *The Tapestry of Saint Joseph.* Philadelphia, Pennsylvania: Apostle Publishing, 1991.

Suarez, Federico. *Joseph of Nazareth.* Princeton, New Jersey: Scepter Publishers, Inc., 1984.

----. *"Thank you for having responded to my call." "Words from the Mother of God at Medjugorje who leads us to her Son."* South Godstone, Surrey: Marian Spring Center, 1997.

Tetlow, Joseph A., S.J. *Ignatius Loyola Spiritual Exercises.* New York: The Crossland Publishing Company, 1992.

----. *The Glories of Saint Joseph.* Traditions Monastiaques, 1997.

----. *The Great Heart of Joseph.* Washington, D.C.: St. Joseph Medal, 1971.

----. *The Little Flower of St. Francis.* Translated by E.M. Blaiklock & A.C. Keys). Ann Arbor, Michigan: Servant Books, 1985.

Thompson, Edward Healy, M.A. *The Life and Glories of Saint Joseph.* Rockford Illinois: TAN Books and Publishers, Inc., 1988.

----. Today With St. Joseph. Washington, D.C.: St. Joseph Medal, 1995.

Two Friends from Medjugorje. *Words from Heaven*. Birmingham. Alabama: Saint James Publishing, 1994.

Urteaga, J. *Man the Saint*. Chicago, Illinois: Scepter Publishers, Ltd., 1963.

Vann, Fr. Joseph, O.F.M. (editor) *Lives of Saints*. New York: John J. Crawley & Co., Inc., 1954.

----. *Vatican*. Vatican City, Italy: Ufficio Vendita Pubblicazioni; Francisco Parafava, 1993.

Walsh, William Thomas. *Our Lady of Fatima*. New York, New York: Bantam Doubleday Dell Publishing Group, Inc., 1954.

Williamson, Hugh Ross. *The Young People's Book of Saints*. New York: Hawthorn Books, Inc., 1962.

----. *Work Today With St. Joseph*. Washington, D.C.: St. Joseph Medal, 1996.

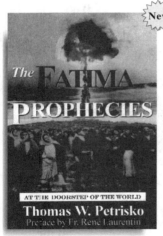

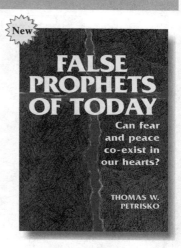

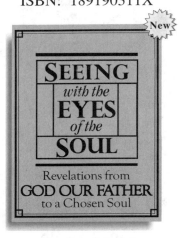